The Wonderful Story of Mother Goose

A Pantomime

Norman Robbins

Samuel French – London
New York – Sydney – Toronto – Hollywood

CHARACTERS

The Fairy Queen
Harmony, the good fairy
Discord, the wicked fairy
Clarence Creep, the village Squire
Jill Goose, the village belle
Colin, her sweetheart
Billy Goose, Jill's elder brother
Sage
Onions } the Squire's bailiffs
Mother Goose, a poor widow
Priscilla, the magic goose
Chorus of **Villagers, Schoolchildren, Fairies, Babes,** etc.

PROLOGUE

The Fairy Queen's Bower

ACT I

SCENE 1   The Village of Merrilea
SCENE 2   A Quiet Street
SCENE 3   The Village School
SCENE 4   A Quiet Street
SCENE 5   The Ballroom of Goose Grange

ACT II

SCENE 1   The Grounds of Goose Grange
SCENE 2   Outside Cheatem Hall
SCENE 3   Beside the Witch's Pool
SCENE 4   A Quiet Street
SCENE 5   The Court of the Fairy Queen
SCENE 6   Back in Merrilea
SCENE 7   The Ballroom of Goose Grange and Finale

MUSICAL NUMBERS

Please read the note on page vi and the Author's Note on
p. vii.

ACT I
No. 1   Villagers
No. 2   Jill, Colin
No. 3   Billy
No. 4   Mother Goose, Jill, Billy, Colin, Sage, Onions,
         Villagers
No. 5   Jill, Colin, Babes
No. 6   Jill, Colin
No. 7   Villagers
No. 8   Billy, Priscilla
No. 9   Company
No. 10   Ballet. Harmony, Fairies

ACT II
No. 11   Villagers
No. 12   Colin, Jill
No. 13   Colin, Jill
No. 14   Mother Goose, Men
No. 15   Ballet. Fairies
No. 16   Dance. Babes, Juniors
No. 17 (optional)   Company
No. 18 (optional)   Dance. Babes *or* Juniors
No. 19   Company

MUSIC

The choice of songs and dance music is left to the individual director. Please read the notice below most carefully:

A licence issued by Samuel French Ltd to perform this play does NOT include permission to use any copyright music in the performance. The notice printed below on behalf of the Performing Right Society should be carefully read.

The following statement concerning the use of music is printed here on behalf of the Performing Right Society Ltd, by whom it was supplied
The permission of the owner of the performing right in copyright music must be obtained before any public performance may be given, whether in conjunction with a play or sketch or otherwise, and this permission is just as necessary for amateur performances as for professional. The majority of copyright musical works (other than oratorios, musical plays and similar dramatico-musical works) are controlled in the British Commonwealth by the PERFORMING RIGHT SOCIETY LTD, 29–33 BERNERS STREET, LONDON W1P 4AA.

The Society's practice is to issue licences authorizing the use of its repertoire to the proprietors of premises at which music is publicly performed, or, alternatively, to the organizers of musical entertainments, but the Society does not require payment of fees by performers as such. Producers or promoters of plays sketches, etc., at which music is to be performed, during or after the play or sketch, should ascertain whether the premises at which their performances are to be given are covered by a licence issued by the Society, and if they are not, should make application to the Society for particulars as to the fee payable.

AUTHOR'S NOTE

The presentation of this pantomime should cause little difficulty to experienced or inexperienced groups. Everything has been kept to the confines of the normal Community Hall, and lighting and props kept to a minimum. Every full stage scene is preceded by a lane-cloth scene, thus allowing plenty of time for setting up behind.

Costuming is traditional children's story-book type, with the exception of the character of Mother Goose, who, once she becomes rich, can wear almost anything outrageous, no matter what period or style.

Additional songs and dances may be added at the discretion of the director, or can be omitted from several parts of the script.

It is suggested, in the Prologue, that the attendant Fairies, etc., are played by the Babes, thus leaving the Junior and Senior Chorus members free for the opening of Scene One. In the Schoolroom scene *all* Chorus members are involved. If men are not available to play the two Evil Spirits of the Mirror in the Ballroom scene, two girls may be used, in which case, dress them in leotards and filmy draperies and omit Mother Goose's line, "I like the supporting pieces." The rest of the show should be self-evident.

The traditional "slap-stick" used in the Schoolroom scene is easily made with two thin strips of wood . . . about 18 inches long, and 1 inch in width . . . secured at one end with tape to create a grip, and a sliver of foam rubber or sponge inserted at the bottom of the V that is formed. About two inches down from the other ends, an elastic cord is fixed to hold the two ends from flying too far apart. When the stick is slapped on a solid surface, it should make a loud noise. If you have not the time or inclination to make one of these, an old-fashioned tawse can be simply made by using a 1½-inch wide piece of buckram, covered with dark felt, and the ends fringed to a depth of about three inches. Both look effective when striking someone, and neither do any harm.

Keep the pace brisk, the music bright, and above all, enjoy yourselves.

Norman Robbins

For

Martin Phillips

A small recognition of his invaluable assistance to me over the years with research and assembly

and

Dathanne (Kerby) E. Kerber

of Illinois, USA, who, to the best of my knowledge, was the first Principal Boy in America in an all-American production of a British Pantomime

PROLOGUE*

The Fairy Queen's Bower

The CURTAIN *rises on a lane cloth depicting the floral bower of the Fairy Queen. This should be lit softly in delicate pastel shades*

The Fairy Queen herself is C, *resplendent in glittering gown and silver crown. In front of her, and to the* R *two small pixies kneel supporting a large golden book. This is open.* R *of the Fairy Queen is the Fairy Harmony. To each side of the two proud principals, fairies, pixies and elves are in tableaux*

Fairy Queen   (*graciously*) Once more the yearly task we face
Of choosing from the human race
Deserving persons to reward
With fairy gifts. Do all accord?

All agree with nods and smiles

(*With satisfaction*) So be it. Now, as well we know,
Full details of all deeds below
On Earth are entered in this book.
(*She indicates it*)
Both Good *and* Bad. (*To Harmony*) Come. Take a look.
Call out those worthy of our blessing.
(*A trifle impatiently*) Quickly now, for time is pressing.

Harmony quickly steps to the book and reads

Harmony There's Widow Twankey and her son, Aladdin. Richard Whittington. Bo-Peep . . . Boy Blue . . . Red Riding Hood. Two tiny Babes lost in a wood. (*She looks appealingly at the Fairy Queen*) All *sorely* needing fairy aid.
Fairy Queen   (*nodding*) I quite agree. Let plans be made
To change their fortunes. Thank you, dear.
Now close the book until *next* year.
(*She turns away as though to exit*)
Harmony (*giving a gasp as she is about to close the book*) Your Majesty. One moment, pray. Oh, dear . . . I scarce know what to say.

All look at her in surprise

Some careless writer long ago has mixed two entries up, and so
For years, alas, we've failed to see our help's been needed *desperately*

All react with dismay

Fairy Queen (*frowning*) It has? By whom? Read out their name.
Harmony   Poor Mother Goose. A widowed dame
                     Of Nursery Land. Her awful plight demands our skills
                        this very night.
                     A poor, hard-working, loving mother ...

   Discord enters L with a sneer on her face

Discord   And a grasping fool. Like ev'ry other.

Everyone reacts

Fairy Queen (*with annoyance*) How *dare* you intrude within my bower?
                     Begone, foolish Discord, or lose your power.
                     I've no need in *my* Court for creatures like you.
Discord   Your pardon, my Queen ... but I think that you *do*.
                     Each year you give blessings to mortals below,
                     But no one *deserves* them, as well you must know.
                     All mortals are greedy. They're selfish and vain.
                     Yet *you* grant them wishes again and again.
                     If *I* were in your shoes, I'd care not a jot
                     For all their entreaties. I'd poison the lot.
                     (*She glares at the audience*)

Everyone reacts with dismay

Harmony (*indignantly*) Your Majesty ...
Fairy Queen (*holding up her hand*) Silence. Enough I have heard. (*To
Discord*) For those words you're banished.

Discord tries to speak

                     (*Sharply*) No. Don't say a *word*.
                     Your vile accusations we've suffered too long.
                     We're tired of your lying.
Discord   They're *not* lies. You're wrong.
                     (*She stamps her foot*)
                     Just give me a chance and I'll prove what I claim.
                     You'll rue your harsh judgement.
Fairies   Why, shame on you. Shame.
Fairy Queen   (*coldly*) Very well, then. This matter we'll settle for good.
                     We'll see if I'm wrong and you're "misunderstood".
                     To Earth you shall go, where your task shall be this ...
                     To persuade ... (*she thinks*) Mother Goose that self-int'rest
                        is bliss.

There is a surprised reaction from the others

                     Succeed and my crown will be placed on *your* head.
                     But fail ... and I promise ... you'll wish you were dead.

Discord   (*delightedly*) There's no fear of failure. I'll do it, you'll see.
Your crown shall be mine and you'll bow down to *me*.
You may as well face it and throw in the tow'l.
I'll tempt Mother Goose . . . by fair means *or foul*.

Discord gives a truly terrible laugh and exits quickly

The assembly look most concerned

Harmony   (*half afraid*) Your Majesty . . . surely you meant but to jest?
Poor, kind, Mother Goose, has been *too long* oppressed.
What chance will she stand against Discord's great power?
I doubt she'll hold out for the space of one hour.
And pardon my asking . . . but was it quite wise
To make Discord the offer of such a great prize?

Fairy Queen (*smiling*) Though it may seem in anger I spoke without
thought,
My aim is that Discord a lesson be taught.
Don't worry, dear Harmony. She'll meet her match.
For to aid Mother Goose, now a rare scheme we'll hatch.
To her cottage on Earth, take Priscilla our Goose.
Give her "certain instructions" . . . and then turn her loose.
We'll show Fairy Discord that good *will* prevail.
Now off on your mission . . . and on with the tale.

The assembled group smile with relief and exit in a flurry as

The Lights quickly fade to a Black-out

ACT I

SCENE 1

The Village of Merrilea

A typical pantomime village setting of quaint houses, cottages and shops, set against a backdrop of distant hills and thick forest. UR *is a tiny, ramshackle cottage with a badly thatched roof and a practical door. This is the home of Mother Goose and her family. Partial views of other buildings can be seen* DR, UL *and* DR

When the scene begins, it is a bright, sunny morning and the Villagers are singing and dancing happily

Song 1

At the end of the song, one of the boys looks off UL *and calls out a warning*

Boy Look out, everyone. Here comes Clarence Creep, the wicked Squire.

Everyone moves aside as Clarence Creep enters with a swagger. He is dressed in Hunting Pink and carries a riding crop. He moves DS

Clarence Three cheers for me. Hip, hip ...
Villagers (*loudly*) Boo.
Clarence (*with annoyance*) Silence, you pathetic pack of polymorphic peasantry. (*He glares at them*) So that's the way you greet your new Lord and Master, is it? Just for that, I've a good mind not to tell you the good news. (*He adopts an aloof posture*)

Everyone looks interested

Girl Good news?
Clarence Yes. As from today, I'm putting your rents up by a pound a week.

All react in dismay

Boy That's not good news.
Clarence It is to *me*. (*He chortles*) That'll teach you to respect your betters. Now clear off, the lot of you ... before I lose my temper.

The Villagers exit with much booing

(*Smirking*) And now to do something *really* nasty. According to the record books, that feeble-minded old faggot, Mother Goose, owes more rent money than the rest of the villagers put together. If it hadn't been for that pretty little daughter of hers, she'd have been tossed into the street years ago. But I'm not so soft-hearted as my late brother. Unless I get the money today, out she goes. Lock, stock and barrel. (*He marches up to the cottage door and knocks loudly*) Come out, you pugnacious, pea-brained parochial parasite. (*He turns away, rubbing his hands in anticipation*)

The cottage door opens and Jill appears. She is a very pretty girl in clean but shabby clothing

Jill (*sweetly*) Good-morning. (*She recognizes his back*) Oh ...

Clarence (*turning quickly to face her*) Mistress Jill. (*He leers*) How delightful to see you.

Jill (*quickly*) If you're looking for mother, Squire Creep, I'm afraid you're out of luck. (*She moves past him* DS) My brother Billy has just taken her down to the Church jumble sale.

Clarence (*aside*) Yes ... and it's the best place for the old crackpot. (*He gives a false laugh*) Your mother, my dear? Why on earth should I be looking for *her*? (*He follows her*) No, no. As a matter of fact ... *you* are the reason for my surprise visit.

Jill Me?

Clarence (*leering*) This very evening, in my stately home, Cheatem Hall, I'm holding a little *soirée*. (*Condescendingly*) That's French for party, in case you don't know ... and I wondered if you'd care to attend? (*Airily*) All the *best* people will be there. The Duke and his Duchess ... the Baron and his Baroness ... the Vicar and his ... er ... *Vixen*. (*Smugly*) Oh, yes. It's going to be a very posh "do", I can assure you.

Jill (*puzzled*) Then why ask me? I'm only a poor village girl.

Clarence True. And of course, you haven't a scrap of breeding in you ... but when it comes to *beauty*, why, there's not a girl in the county to equal you (*He drops to one knee in front of her*)

> Curly-locks, curly-locks, wilt thou be mine?
> Thou shalt not clean dishes, nor yet feed the swine.
> But sit on a cushion and sew a fine seam,
> And feed upon strawberries, sugar and cream.

Jill (*trying not to laugh*) Aren't you forgetting something, Squire Creep? I'm already engaged to your nephew, Colin. As soon as he arrives back from London we're going to name the day.

Clarence (*jumping up in a temper*) So ... you spurn my advances, do you? Very well, then. As soon as I've summoned my bailiffs, it's into the streets with you. We'll see how long it takes for you to come to your senses. (*He calls loudly*) Bailiffs. Bailiffs. (*Fuming*) Never around when I need them. (*He calls again*) Bailiffs.

He exits angrily DR *still shouting*

Jill (*worried*) Oh, dear. I'd better find mother and warn her.

Colin enters UL *a broad smile on his face. He wears tunic and tights, and carries a stick over his shoulder from which hangs a knotted bag*

Colin Jill.

Jill (*turning and seeing him*) Colin.

They hurry to each other and embrace

Oh, thank goodness you're back.

Colin (*teasing her*) Don't say you actually missed me these past few weeks? (*He tosses his stick and bag to the ground*)

Jill Of course I've missed you ... but that's not the only reason I'm glad to see you. It's that wicked uncle of yours again.

Colin (*groaning*) Oh, no. What's he been up to *this* time? He's been nothing but trouble since he arrived in the village.

Jill He came round here a few minutes ago and asked me to marry him. Then when I refused, he threatened to have us thrown out of the cottage. What are we going to do?

Colin Don't worry, Jill. As long as you keep paying the rent, he can't do a thing.

Jill That's just the trouble. We *haven't* been paying it. (*Sadly*) What little money we have is spent on food, and there's hardly enough of *that* for us to live on. (*She turns away*) Oh, Colin. I'm so miserable.

Colin (*smiling*) Cheer up. You've got nothing to worry about. You won't be turned out of your cottage, I promise.

Jill How can you say that? We're all penniless.

Colin Not any more. During my stay in London, I got a job in Fitzwarren's Store. Looking after the place whilst the Alderman and his daughter were abroad. When they came back he paid me a *hundred pounds*. Now I can pay all the rent money your mother owes and there'll still be enough left for us to get married with.

Jill (*with delight*) Oh, Colin. That's the best news I've heard in my entire life. I can't wait to tell mother. She'll be so relieved.

Colin I can't imagine Uncle Clarence being very pleased about it, though. (*He grins*) He'll be furious.

Jill What a pity *he's* the Squire of Merrilea. I don't understand why your father didn't make a Will leaving everything to you.

Colin No more do I. But Uncle Clarence turned up and claimed everything was his, and I'm still under age ... (*He shrugs*) Still ... I'm not going to worry myself about it. I may not have wealth and rank, but I do have *you* and that's enough to keep me happy for the rest of my life.

Jill and Colin sing

Song 2

At the end of the song they exit into the cottage

As they do so, Billy Goose enters DL. *He is dressed in very "loud" clothing, patched and ragged, and carries a large teddy bear*

Billy (*singing*) Me and my teddy bear ... he's got no eyes and he's got no hair ... (*He sees the audience*) Ooooooh. Hallo, boys and girls. (*Assumed half-hearted reaction*) Is anybody there? (*Loudly*) Hallo, boys and girls. (*Warmer reaction*) Oh, *dear*. Shall I go off and come back on again? (*Disgustedly*) You can do better than *that*, can't you? I mean ... you've not all got sore throats? You *have*? Well ... I can soon fix that. (*He gets* *out a packet of cough sweets and tosses individual sweets out to various points of the audience*) Now all you people who got one ... just one suck each, then pass it on to the person sitting at the side of you. And you lot do the same. If there's anything left over when you've finished, hand them to the programme sellers at the interval. We can use them again tomorrow night. Right. Come on. All together. (*He shouts loudly*) Hallo, boys and girls. (*Audience reaction*) There ... that's better. Now then ... I'm Billy Goose, but everybody round here calls me silly Billy ... I can't think why ... and this (*he indicates the teddy*) is (*he names the local railway station*) my Teddy. I call him that, because he's a relation of Paddington Bear. Of course ... I have to keep my eye on him. You see, with him having a famous cousin, people keep trying to steal him from me. Aren't they naughty? And every time I put him down, somebody tries to grab him. I can't sleep for thinking about it ... but tonight ... seeing as how you're all there watching ... will you keep an eye on him for me? (*Audience reaction*) You will? Oh, smashing. Now I'll tell you what. I'm going to put Teddy over here. (*He places it by the proscenium arch R*) ... and if anyone comes near him, I want you to shout "Billy" at the top of your voices, and I'll hear you and come running. Can you do that? (*Audience reaction*) All right, then. We'll have a little practice. I'll pretend to be a nasty old tea-leaf who's trying to pinch my Teddy, and you have to warn me. Are you ready? (*He coaches the audience into the warning*) Oh, smashing. I know he'll be safe now. Right ... we can get on with the story. (*He takes a deep breath*) My name's Billy Goose and I live in that little cottage (*he indicates it*) with my mother and my little sister Jill. And ... oooh, we are poor. We've got no money at all. In fact, when me and Jill were babies, Mum couldn't even afford to buy talcum powder. We just had to rough it. And none of us have got jobs. Well ... *I* had a job once, but I had to leave it because of illness. The Boss got sick of me. I was ever so upset. I jumped onto my skateboard and went racing down the street at seventy miles an hour. All of a sudden, this policeman stopped me. "Here," he said "this is a one-way street." I said, "I'm only going one way." He said, "Yes ... and it's the wrong one. Didn't you see the arrows?" I said, "I didn't even see the Indians." He said, "Come on. I want you to blow into this little bag." I said, "What for?" He said, "'Cos me chips are too hot." (*He laughs*) Mind you ... I had a very upsetting experience yesterday. I ran over a little dog's tail and chopped it right off. Thwack (*He winces*) Anyway, I soon fixed it. I took him into a retailers. (*He chortles*) Right. I'll see you later, kids. I'm going in now to get some sleep. I didn't get much last night. I plugged my electric blanket into the toaster and kept popping out of bed every two minutes. (*He sings*)

Song 3

At the end of the song, Bill exits into the cottage

As he does so, Sage and Onions, the Squire's Bailiffs hurry on, both looking anxious

Sage (*breathlessly*) Cor, that was a narrow escape, Onions. I thought Squire Creep had spotted us for the minute.

Onions (*wheezing*) Me too. Oh, I wish we'd never agreed to be his Bailiffs. All we seem to do is toss people out of their houses. He's a real nasty piece of work, he is.

Sage Yes. I should have remembered what an old skinflint he was before I took the job. Do you know ... last Christmas I called round at his house and told him I was collecting for the Old People's Home. And guess what he gave me?

Onions What?

Sage His Grandma and Grandad.

Onions (*sighing*) Oh, I wish I could go back to my old job. I used to be a chef in one of those motorway cafés. You know ... a stale doughnut and a slice of coffee for five pounds. But I had to leave when the gas cooker went out.

Sage (*puzzled*) Why was that? You could have lit it again, couldn't you?

Onions No. It went out through the roof. Mind you, I was a terrible chef. I couldn't boil water without burning it. Everything I cooked tasted horrible and the customers were always complaining.

Sage Why didn't you try a recipe book?

Onions Oh ... I never thought of that. What do they taste like?

Sage Honestly. You're as thick as two short planks, you are. Anyway, I can't stand here all morning talking to you. I've got an appointment at the dentist's.

Onions Why? Have you got toothache?

Sage No, but all my teeth are going yellow.

Onions Don't you use toothpaste?

Sage Why should I? None of my teeth are loose. Anyway, I can't really afford to go to the dentist. We haven't been paid since we started this job. If anybody tried to pick *my* pockets right now, all they'd get is practice.

Onions I had *my* pocket picked once ... by a man with only one finger.

Sage (*with interest*) What did he get?

Onions A polo mint.

Sage Well ... it's no use us standing here in the village square. If Creepy Clarence comes back he might see us. Let's go down to (*he names a local pub*) and play cards with the landlord.

Onions Oh, no. Not me. I don't play cards with *him* any more.

Sage Why not?

Onions Would *you* play cards with a man who cheats and keeps all the aces up his sleeve?

Sage (*indignantly*) I certainly wouldn't.

Onions No. And neither will he.

Sage hits Onions over the head with his hat and they exit DL

As they do so, the Lights dim

Discord enters UL *with a cruel laugh. She moves* C

Discord Earth at last. How often I've dreamed of this moment. Free from

the prying eyes and tattling tongues of those self-satisfied minions of the Fairy Queen. (*Fiercely*) I'll show her that Discord's powers are not to be sneered at. Not only will I bring Mother Goose to her knees, I'll bring misery and pain to anyone who crosses my path. (*She laughs*)
    But now I'll away ... foolproof plans to define. ...
    And the Fairy Queen's crown very soon shall be mine.

Discord cackles with laughter and exits L

As she does, the Lights go up

Mother Goose enters R. *She is old, plain and shabby, dressed in clothes even a tramp would shy away from. Nevertheless she has an almost permanent smile on her face and is warm-hearted and generous. She carries a battered, old, shopping bag*

Mother Goose (*singing in a very cracked voice*) Someday he'll come along ... the man I love ... (*She sees the audience*) Oh, hallo, dears. (*She beams at them*) Welcome to Merrilea. Goose is the name. Mother Goose. Well, well, well ... what a lovely looking lot you are. (*She calls offstage*) Put the lights up, love, so I can get a better look at them.

The House Lights go up to full

(*Turning to face the audience*) That's better ... (*She shrieks*) Ohhhhhhhh. (*She calls offstage*) Take 'em down again. Take 'em down.

The House Lights are quickly lowered

(*Clutching at her heart*) Oh, you don't want to give me shocks like that. A woman in my condition. I nearly had a conniption. All those *eyes*. It was like looking at a fishmonger's slab. I could see one old trout in the fifth row. Mind you ... it's not that I've got anything against fish. I've got one myself. Ever so talented it is. Every night after supper it pops out of its bowl and plays the piano for us. (*With surprise*) What are you laughing for? You've heard of a piano Tuna, haven't you? (*She fishes in her bag*) Here ... I must tell you ... I've just been to the jumble sale. Talk about bargains. Look what I've bought. (*She extracts a pair of old odd gloves*) Doe-skin gloves. Made of real dough, too, so if I don't wear them, I can bake 'em into a loaf of bread. Of course ... they're both for the same hand, so I can only wear them one at a time, but that's what's so good about them. They'll last twice as long, won't they? (*She rummages inside the bag again*) I bought a dress as well. One of those modern ones with a lintel round the architraves and not much material up here ... (*she indicates her bustline*) The vicar's wife said it was a "Golfing Dress". The only trouble is, every time I bend down, I'm a bit scared in case my niblicks fall out. Oh, but I do love jumble sales, don't you? I met my late husband at a jumble sale. There I was ... minding my own business when suddenly I caught his eye. It had fallen out when somebody bumped against him. He rushed straight over and kissed me on both cheeks. I wouldn't have minded, but I was picking up my handbag at the time. Talk about love at first sight. He took one look at my face ... and three weeks

later ... when he came out of the asylum ... we were married. (*She sighs*)
Oh, girls ... I'll never forget that wedding day. I've *tried*, but I'll never
forget it. Well you know how it is? I wanted to look really beautiful and
slim for him, so I decided to go and have a Turkish Bath. So off I went
and I found this marvellous place ... all white tiles and thick, thick steam.
In I went and took all my clothes off and lay down on the slab. Then
suddenly the steam cleared and I found myself in a Fish and Chip shop.
Oh, I've never moved so fast since my granny iced the cake with Ex-lax. I
was out of that door and down the street like a rocket. I shot past two old
men on the pavement, and one turned to the other and said. "Here ... did
you see what *she* was wearing?" and the other one said, "No, but
whatever it was, it needed ironing."

Clarence Creep enters UL

Clarence Aha ... (*He strides towards her*)
Mother Goose (*turning*) Oh ... it's (*she names a well-known unpopular man*)
Clarence (*snarling*) I want my money, you nematoidical, neanderthalic,
  neurotic old nincompoop.
Mother Goose (*to the audience*) Oh, I hate that word "old".
Clarence Hand it over now, or you're in for a very nasty surprise.
Mother Goose How much do I owe you?
Clarence Fifty pounds.
Mother Goose Fifty pounds? For a tiny little cottage like that? The
  kitchen's so small I can only use condensed milk. (*Stricken*) Oh, whatever
  am I going to do. I can't afford to give you that much.
Clarence Very well, then. Just to prove I'm not as bad as everyone thinks I
  am ... I'll forget about half of it.
Mother Goose Oh, how kind of you. And just to show how grateful I am,
  I'll forget the other half.
Clarence (*snorting*) Bah. You, madam, are next to an idiot.
Mother Goose Would you like me to move?
Clarence Yes ... into the street. (*He calls*) Bailiffs. Bailiffs.

Sage and Onions appear UL

Toss this old faggot into the street at once.
Mother Goose (*startled*) Eh? You can't do that. (*She lets out a wail*)
  Ooooooooooh.

The Villagers come hurrying on, all agog

Villagers What is it? What's happening, etc. etc.

Billy and Jill appear in the cottage doorway

Jill (*with concern*) Mother. What's wrong? (*She hurries to her side*)
Mother Goose (*sobbing*) We're being turned out of our little cottage.
Billy (*coming down*) Well ... I'll be nationalized.
Villagers (*to Clarence*) Boo, shame, hiss, etc.
Clarence (*loudly*) Quiet, you repulsive, rebellious rabble. This old harridan
  owes me fifty pounds, and as she can't pay it, out she goes.

Jill Fifty pounds?

Clarence That includes the rates, of course.

Billy But we haven't got rates. Only a few little mayce.

Jill (*to Clarence*) Couldn't you give us time to pay?

Clarence How much time?

Mother Goose About ten years. (*She sobs*) I haven't got fifty pence, let alone fifty pounds.

Colin enters from the cottage

Colin But *I* have. Don't worry, Mother Goose. I'll pay the rent for you, then he can't throw you out. (*He hands her some pound notes*)

Clarence (*fuming*) Curses. What are *you* doing back here? I thought you'd gone to London to seek your fortune.

Colin So I had, but as you can see, I'm back in Merrilea and just in time to stop your little game. Now take your pet monkeys (*he indicates Sage and Onions*) and clear off.

Clarence Bah. I'll remember this. No one gets the better of Clarence Creep. (*He turns to go*)

Mother Goose (*quickly*) Here ... don't go without your rent money. And I'll pay you in front of all these witnesses so you can't say I haven't done it. Stick your measly mucky mauler out.

Clarence holds out his hand

(*Counting*) One, two, three, four, five ... (*she pauses*) How many weeks rent did I owe you?

Clarence (*snarling*) Ten.

Mother Goose Ten?

Clarence (*firmly*) Ten.

Mother Goose (*counting*) Eleven, twelve, thirteen, fourteen ... (*She pauses*) And how many other people in the village owe you money?

Clarence (*sourly*) Thirty-six.

Mother Goose (*with amazement*) Thirty-six?

Clarence Thirty-six.

Mother Goose (*counting*) Thirty-seven, thirty-eight, thirty-nine, forty ... (*she pauses*) I suppose you're owed quite a large amount then?

Clarence I certainly am. Even after *you've* paid me, I'm still owed sixty-eight pounds.

Mother Goose (*with amazement*) Sixty-eight pounds?

Clarence Sixty-eight pounds.

Mother Goose (*impressed*) Sixty-eight pou ... (*she breaks off suddenly*) Here ... just a minute. I only owed you fifty. I've paid you eighteen too much. I'd better have that back, if you don't mind. (*She snatches the notes off him and quickly counts them*) Hey ... there's only thirteen here. You owe me another five. (*She holds out her hand*) Hand it over.

Clarence (*with confusion*) Eh? Oh. Er ... yes. Yes. You're quite right. I'm terribly sorry. (*He gets out a five pound note and hands it to her*) I do apologize.

Billy Yes ... you've got to watch his sort, haven't you boys and girls?

The Villagers agree

Mother Goose (*beaming*) Well. Now that that's settled, here's five pounds to buy everybody an ice cream. (*She hands the fiver to a Villager*)

The Villagers react with delight

    (*To Billy, Jill and Colin*) And *we'll* go inside and have a nice cup of tea. (*To Clarence*) Bysie-bye, Squire.

    Mother Goose, Billy, Jill and Colin exit into the cottage

    The Villagers exit happily at all exits

Clarence and the Bailiffs are left alone

Clarence (*baffled*) Just a minute. Just a minute. (*He looks at his hand*) I don't understand. (*He realizes*) I've been diddled. (*Furiously*) Come back you old twister. (*Fuming*) Right. That's done it. The next time I see her, she's out on her ear. (*He glares at the Bailiffs*) This is all *your* fault, you bone-headed bird brains. I'm deducting that fiver from your wages. Come on.

    Angrily he storms off UL, *followed by the dazed Sage and Onions*

As they exit, the Lights dim slightly

    Harmony enters DR. *She is followed by Priscilla the Goose*

Both are picked out in a white follow spot

Harmony   (*moving* C) On pinioned wing, from Fairy portal,
                Comes this magic Goose immortal;
                And, by virtue of her power,
                Mother Goose's darkest hour
                Shall be lightened. This I vow.
                So come, Priscilla . . . take your bow.

Priscilla bows to the audience

                Your task begins. Delay no more
                But knock on yonder cottage door;
                And never fear, I'll stay close by
                To keep an ever watchful eye.

    She exits with a flourish of her wand

Priscilla waddles up to the door, and with her beak, knocks loudly. She cocks her head, but there is no response from within. She knocks again. Still no response

    Priscilla moves away from the door and exits around the back of the cottage

    As she does so, the door opens and Mother Goose peers out

Mother Goose That's funny? I could have sworn I heard somebody knocking. (*She comes out of the cottage and moves downstage*) I was just having a sit down. (*She turns to go back upstage and we can see her skirt* *tucked into the waistband of her bloomers*) Well . . . there's nobody here. I may as well go back in.

Priscilla re-enters from the other side of the cottage

(*Startled*) Oh . . . it's Orville.

Priscilla shakes her head

No it's not. It's a goose. A great big beautiful goose. Well, well, well. I wonder who *you* belong to?

Priscilla shakes her head

(*With surprise*) You don't belong to anybody? (*Worriedly*) Oh, dear . . . You're not wandering around all on your own, are you?

Priscilla nods

And was it you who just knocked on my door?

Priscilla nods

There. And I thought it might have been opportunity.

Priscilla nods

It *was*? Is that your name, then? Opportunity?

Priscilla shakes her head

Well what is it, then? Come on. Whisper it in my ear.

Priscilla whispers in Mother Goose's ear

Cilla. Oh, I say. Here . . . you're not Cilla Black, are you?

Priscilla shakes her head

No. No.

Priscilla whispers again

But you can sing a lot better. (*She laughs*) Oh, you saucy old goose. You'd better not let her agent hear you saying that.

Priscilla whispers again

Oh . . . it was her agent that told you. Well what is your name *really*?

Priscilla whispers again

Priscilla. Well, what a pretty name. Oh, here . . . I'd better introduce *my*self, hadn't I? (*She curtsies*) Mother Goose. (*She rises again*)

Priscilla curtsies back and Mother Goose curtsies again. Priscilla curtsies back and Mother Goose curtsies again, bobbing up and down three times in quick succession

Oops, I've got my suspenders caught in my shoe buckles. (*She untangles herself*) Well . . . it's been very nice meeting you, Priscilla, but it's time you were running along. You don't want to be late for your dinner, do you? Bye-bye.

Priscilla stays where she is

Go on. Off you pop. (*She smiles*) Shoo. Shoo. (*She waves her apron at Priscilla*) Go on. (*Desperately*) Paxo.

Priscilla remains looking at her

Well you can't stand outside my house all day. Haven't you got a home to go to?

Priscilla shakes her head

No? (*With concern*) Oh, you poor thing. I never realized. Here ... well don't you worry. We haven't much food and we've got no money, but at least we've still got a roof over our heads. How would you like to come and live with Jill, Billy and me in our little cottage?

Priscilla nods her head and does a little dance

Oooh, smashing. Well that's where we live. In you go and find yourself a nice warm spot to sleep in.

Priscilla waddles into the cottage

(*To the audience*) Oh ... isn't she *bootiful*? I bet Bernard Matthews wishes his turkeys grew like that.

There is a general entrance of Villagers

(*Excitedly*) Here, everybody, listen. You'll never guess what's happened. I've just found a great big goose called Priscilla and I can't wait to tell you how pretty she is. She's got white feathers and a big yellow beak and ...

Clarence enters with the Bailiffs

Clarence (*pushing his way through*) Ahaaaa.
Mother Goose (*sighing*) Look out. The river's back.
Clarence River?
Mother Goose Yes. The biggest part of you is your mouth.
Clarence Bah. (*To his Bailiffs*) Throw her out.
Mother Goose (*wailing*) Ohhhhhhh.

The Villagers hiss and boo

Clarence (*ignoring them*) And what's that teddy bear doing littering up the street? I'll toss it in the dustbin. (*He moves towards it*)

Audience reaction

Billy comes rushing out of the cottage

Billy Keep your hands off my teddy.

Clarence turns away with a snarl

(*To the audience*) Thanks, kids. (*To his Mum*) What's going on, Mum?

Mother Goose He's trying to turn us out of the cottage again. (*She sobs*)

    Colin and Jill enter from the cottage

Colin Is that so? (*He faces Clarence*) Then I'm afraid you're out of luck, Uncle Clarence. This time there'll be no practical joking. I'll pay you the rent money myself.

Clarence (*snarling*) Too late, you interfering popinjay. Out they go whether you like it or not. First thing tomorrow morning I'm having the whole place demolished and the site turned into a car park.

Billy Don't be daft. Cars haven't been invented yet.

Clarence They will have been by the time it's ready. I've asked (*he names the local council*) to do the job.

There is a great cackling from inside the cottage

Jill (*startled*) What's that?

Mother Goose It's me new lodger. Priscilla. Quick, Billy. Go in and see if she's all right.

    Billy dashes into the cottage

Billy (*off*) Ooooooh.

Everyone looks at each other

    Billy comes dashing out again carrying a large gold egg

It's a golden egg. She's laid a golden egg.

Everyone reacts with surprise and astonishment

There is more cackling from inside the cottage

Sage Sounds like she's laying another.

Everyone but Clarence gets excited

Billy Here, Mum. Hold this. (*He hands her the egg*)

    Billy dashes back into the cottage

There is a loud thud from inside

Billy (*off*) Oooooooooooooh.

    Billy comes out carrying a much larger egg of gold

There is a big reaction from the crowd

Mother Goose (*weakly*) I don't believe it.

Jill hurries to Billy and takes the egg

As she does so, there is even louder cackling from inside

Onions Blimey. She's at it again.

    Billy dashes back into the cottage

There is a thud that knocks everyone staggering

Billy (*off*) Oooooooooooooooh.

Billy comes staggering out with an immense egg of gold

Colin leaps to help him

Jill (*delightedly*) Mother. Our fortune's made. We're rich.

Mother Goose bursts into tears

Don't *cry*, mother. Priscilla's just laid a fortune for us.

Mother Goose I know. I'm thinking about the poor Mayor. It's only last week the paper said he'd laid a foundation stone weighing two tons ... and *that* was *square*. (*She winces*)

Colin Just think. From now on you can buy anything you want.

Mother Goose Yes ... and we owe it all to Priscilla. Where is the little darling?

Priscilla comes shyly out of the cottage

(*Hugging her*) Oh, you're the most wonderful goose there ever was. (*To Clarence*) You can have your tumbledown old cottage. From now on we'll have money to burn and we're going to live in the biggest, poshest, house in the whole wide world. (*To the cottage*) Sorry, little cottage ... you've been very good to us, but the Goose family is going up in the world.

All cheer

Mother Goose, Jill, Billy, Colin, Sage, Onions and the Villagers sing

Song 4

As the song goes on Clarence storms off in a temper

At the end of the song, the Lights fade on the general celebration and the front runners come in

SCENE 2

A Quiet Street

Discord enters L in a temper

Discord So that stupid Fairy Harmony hopes to outwit me with the aid of our magic goose, does she? We'll see about that.

> O'er Mother Goose a spell I'll weave
> And cause her foolish heart to grieve.
> She'll lose her sunny nature
> And bad temper's sure to flare.
> Just watch her friends forsake her.
> Hah ... she'll end up in despair.
> So though for just a moment things
> Seem very bright and gay,

> Her happiness without a doubt
> I mean to snatch away.

She roars with laughter, then notices the teddy

Hallo ... what's this? (*She moves towards it*)

Audience reaction

Discord quickly exits L

Billy rushes on R *in a very "loud" costume*

Billy Get your hands off my Teddy. (*To the audience*) Thanks kids. Here
... isn't it smashing being rich? I can buy anything I like now. I went into
the pet shop this morning to buy a dog. You know ... one of those hairy
ones like they have in the Dulux adverts. I said to the man behind the
counter, "Here ... how much are them dogs?" He said, "They're two
hundred pounds apiece." I said, "That's no use to me. I want a whole
one."

Clarence enters L

Clarence Ah, Billy Goose. The very man.

Billy (*startled*) Eh?

Clarence I wonder if you could lend me a ten p coin. I'd like to phone a
friend.

Billy Here. Take twenty p and phone them *all*. (*He laughs*)

Clarence (*trying to control himself*) I suppose you think you're somebody
now you're rolling in money, but I'll tell you this. Money means nothing
unless you have the breeding to go with it. I, for instance, recently paid a
fortune to have my Family Tree looked up.

Billy Yes, and now you're paying another one to have it *hushed* up. You're
nothing but an old snob, you are. You won't even eat a hot-dog unless it's
been registered with the Kennel Club.

Clarence Bah.

Billy Here ... I'll tell you what, though. You might be able to give me some
advice.

Clarence (*suspiciously*) Advice?

Billy Yes. I mean ... we've never had any money before, so we don't know
much about it. Can you tell us how to get on in business?

Clarence Ah, well. (*He laughs mockingly*) I must admit that there *is* a little
secret attached to my success.

Billy (*excitedly*) What is it? What is it?

Clarence (*grandly*) Brains, dear boy. Brains. You should eat more *fish*.

Billy Fish? Oh, you're having me on, aren't you? (*To the audience*) He's
having me on. You don't eat fish to get brains, do you? (*Audience
reaction*) You *do*? Honestly?

Clarence But of course ... and as it so happens ... by a strange coincidence
... I have a special kind of fish on my person ... already cooked for my
lunch. Give me two hundred pounds, and it's yours. All you have to do is
eat it, and you'll develop brains.

Billy You're on. (*He gets out a wad of notes and gives them to Clarence*) Here's your two hundred.

Clarence And here's your fish. (*He gets out a small foil wrapped "fish" and hands it over*)

Billy (*unwrapping it*) Oooh, smashing. (*He holds it up by its tail*) Past my lips and past my gums . . . look-out stomach, here it comes. (*He swallows it*)

Clarence (*when he's finished it*) Well . . . do you notice any difference?

Billy (*thinking*) No. (*Puzzled*) But I've just realized . . . wasn't two hundred pounds a bit pricey for a little bit of fish like that?

Clarence You see? You're developing brains already. (*He laughs*)

Clarence exits L

Billy realizes he's been tricked and chases off after him

As he does so, Colin and Jill enter R. *Both are much more smartly dressed*

Jill (*happily*) Oh, Colin. I can hardly believe it. We've got so much money now, we don't know what to do with it.

Colin (*laughing*) I wouldn't say that, Jill. Your mother's finding *plenty* of ways to get rid of it. She's buying presents for everyone in the village, giving thousands of pounds to charity, and arranging the biggest celebration party the country's ever seen. She's the best loved person in England.

Jill Well . . . at least until tomorrow morning.

Colin (*puzzled*) How do you mean?

Jill She's bought the old village schoolhouse and first thing in the morning she's going to open it up again with herself as Headmistress.

Colin But it hasn't been open for years. We couldn't afford a teacher.

Jill That's why she's doing it. She wants everyone to have a chance to learn how to read and write and to do arithmetic.

Colin Well, it's a marvellous idea, but I wonder how the children are going to like it?

Jill (*looking off* L) Here they come now. Let's ask them.

The Babes enter L *looking downcast*

Colin Oh . . . I don't think there's any need. Just look at their faces. (*To the Babes*) Hallo, children.

Babes (*dully*) Hallo, Colin. Hallo, Jill.

Colin I take it you've heard the news. (*They nod*) Cheer up. It's not the end of the world. You might even find you'll like it.

Girl But we've never been to school before.

Boy No. And we don't want to go, either.

Jill (*with concern*) But it's very important to go to school. It's the best way of learning lots of wonderful things and meeting new friends.

Girl Did *you* have to go to school, Jill?

Jill Of course I did. So did Colin. And they were the happiest days of my life.

Colin They certainly were.

Boy Oh, well. In that case, we'll give it a try.

Jill, Colin and the Babes sing

Song 5

At the end of the song all exit as
The Lights fade to Black-out

SCENE 3

The Village School

A classroom. Teacher's desk is UR and on it is a large hand-bell, a conical "Dunce" cap and a slap-stick cane. Just above the desk is a large blackboard on an easel. On the blackboard is chalked a stick-like caricature of a teacher in a mortarboard hat. Below the board, on the rest, are chalks and a blackboard eraser. Two long school benches are opposite the desk, one behind the other and angled C. A shorter bench is in front of these and this is constructed like a letter F face down, so that anyone sitting on the legless end will be tipped to the floor if the other end is not weighted

When the scene begins, it is bedlam. Paper darts are zooming about the room. Two boys are playing conkers, whilst others fire pea-shooters, paper pellets from wooden rulers, or simply race around shouting. Girls play "Ring-a-ring o' roses", yelling the rhyme at the top of their voices, and others are skipping, blowing bubbles, and playing with dolls. Under the shouts and cries, music is playing a spirited version of "Boys and Girls Come Out to Play"

Suddenly Mother Goose bursts onto the stage wearing her cap and gown over her costume. She takes in the scene, grabs the handbell and rings it loudly

With much noise and excitement, the children hurry to their seats on the long benches, sit, and look at her expectantly

She replaces the bell on the desk

Mother Goose (*sweetly*) Good-morning, children.
All Good-morning, teacher.
Mother Goose (*beaming*) Welcome to the Goose Academy of Educational Excellence. I am your Headmistress, Madam de Goosey, and I'd just like to say . . .

A very small boy strolls in R and crosses L

   (*Spotting him*) Hoy. Hoy . . . Tom Thumb.
Boy (*turning to look at her*) You talking to me, missis?
Mother Goose (*taken aback*) Am I . . . (*recovering*) Yes, I am, you pint-sized little perisher. What excuse have you got for being late?
Boy I was throwing peanuts in the river.
Mother Goose (*lost for words, then recovering*) Go and sit down.

The boy crosses to the long benches and sits

As I was saying . . .

Sage and Onions enter R dressed as schoolboys

Sage⎫
Onions⎭ (*together*) Morning, teacher. (*They begin to move L*)

Mother Goose Just a minute. Just a minute. And where do you think you two have been?

Sage⎫
Onions⎭ (*together*) Throwing peanuts in the river.

Mother Goose (*taken aback*) Oh . . . (*recovering*) Well don't come in here late again. Sit down.

They go to the small bench and sit on the "safe" end

Now then . . . as I was saying . . .

Another small boy comes in R and heads L

(*With great sarcasm*) Excuse me.

Boy (*turning to look at her*) Yes, miss?

Mother Goose I don't suppose that by any strange quirk of fate *you've* been throwing peanuts in the river?

Boy Oh, *no*, Miss. I *am* Peanuts.

Mother Goose (*weakly*) Go and sit down.

The boy goes to the long benches and sits

(*Very quickly*) As I was saying . . . (*she glances round at the door*) As I was saying . . . the first thing we're going to do today is . . . (*She spots the teddy*) Whose is that teddy? Come on. Own up. (*No reaction*) Teddy bears are *not* allowed in school. I shall put him in the toy cupboard till going home time. (*She crosses to the Teddy*)

Audience reaction

Billy enters dressed as a schoolboy and very untidy

Billy Get your hands off my Teddy. (*To the audience*) Thanks, kids. (*He recognizes his mother*) Oh . . . (*weakly*) Hallo, mum.

Mother Goose Don't you "Hallo, mum" me, Billy Goose. You should have been here at nine o'clock.

Billy Why? What happened?

Mother Goose (*heavily*) If it isn't too much trouble, would you mind telling us why you're walking into this classroom five minutes late?

Billy It's easy. I was following the Highway Code.

Mother Goose How could that make you late?

Billy Well, there's a sign down the road that says "School. Go slow," so I did.

Everybody laughs

Mother Goose (*crossly*) Silence. (*To Billy*) Put this dunce cap on and sit down. (*She hands him the cap*)

Billy puts it on before he sits on the "unsafe" end of the short bench

Now then ... the first lesson this morning will be arithmetic.

All groan loudly

Everybody get your pencils out.

Billy (*standing*) Here, miss. I ain't got no pencil.

Mother Goose I beg your pudding? You *ain't* got no pencil?

Billy That's right.

Mother Goose (*heavily*) You *haven't* got no pencil. (*Expanding*) He hasn't got no pencil. She hasn't got no pencil. They haven't got no pencils.

Billy Blimey. Ain't nobody got one?

Mother Goose (*defeated*) Oh, sit down and shut up.

Billy sits again, looking baffled

Mother Goose moves up to the blackboard and cleans it

Now ... can everybody see the blackboard?

Sage No, miss.

Mother Goose No? Have your eyes been checked lately?

Sage No, miss. They've always been brown.

Everybody laughs

Mother Goose picks up the chalk and writes 6 + 4 = on the blackboard

Mother Goose Now what is the total of six plus four?

Sage (*standing*) Eleven.

All applaud him

Mother Goose (*with annoyance*) That's the wrong answer. Six and four is *ten*.

Onions (*still sitting*) No it isn't. Five and five is ten.

Mother Goose Who said that?

Onions Me, miss. (*He stands*)

Billy is tipped to the floor

All laugh

Mother Goose (*to Billy: annoyed*) What are you doing down there?

Billy Getting up.

The bench is placed back in position

Mother Goose (*sharply*) Everybody sit down again.

All sit as before

Now then ... it's quite obvious to me that none of you know anything at all about numbers, so we'd better do some practising. How many fingers and thumbs have you got on both hands?

All Ten, miss.

Mother Goose And what would you have if I chopped three of them off?

Billy No more piano lessons. (*He laughs*)

All laugh with him

Mother Goose (*with annoyance*) Who said that?
All Billy Goose.
Mother Goose (*grimly*) Right. Come out here, you. (*She gets the slap-stick cane*)

Reluctantly Billy stands and goes to her

Bend over.

Billy bends over facing her

No, not like that, you fool. Hold this and I'll show you. (*She gives Billy the stick*) Like this. (*She demonstrates*)
Billy You want me to stick my bottom out like that?
Mother Goose Yes I do.
Billy And what are you going to do with this? (*He flexes the stick*)
Mother Goose I'm going to smack you with it.
Billy Like this? (*He smacks her*)
Mother Goose Owwwww. (*She jumps up and snatches the stick from him*) You little monster. (*She grabs him*) Come here. (*She bends him down and canes him*)
Billy Owwwww. (*He rubs his bottom*)
Mother Goose Now get back to your place.

Billy limps back to his seat and gingerly sits

Right. Now supposing I tore a piece of paper into four ... what would I have?
All Quarters.
Mother Goose And if I tore it into eight?
All Eighths.
Mother Goose Into sixteen?
Onions (*standing*) Sixteenths.
Mother Goose And if I tore it into thousands of pieces?
Sage (*standing*) Confetti.

The bench tips and Billy goes flying again

All laugh

Mother Goose (*with annoyance*) Who said that?
All Billy Goose.
Billy (*struggling to his feet*) Eh? I never.
Mother Goose Come here. (*She picks up the stick*)
Billy But ... but ...
Mother Goose Bend over.

Still protesting Billy bends over and she canes him

Meanwhile Sage and Onions replace the bench and sit

Billy Owwwwwww. (*He rubs his bottom and heads back to his seat painfully*)

Mother Goose (*muttering*) I don't know what's got into everybody today. (*She puts the stick down*) It's worse than (*she names a local school*) Has anybody here ever been to school before?
Onions (*standing*) Please, teacher. I have.
Mother Goose Oh, that's something, anyway.
Onions But I got sent home because the boy in front of me started smoking.
Mother Goose (*baffled*) Why did they send *you* home?
Onions It was me that set him on fire. (*He sits again*)

All laugh

Mother Goose (*incensed*) That's done it. That's done it. Stand up all the idiots in this classroom.

For a moment no one moves, then Billy stands

Oh ... so you're an idiot, are you?
Billy No ... but I didn't like to see you standing up there on your own.
Mother Goose (*spluttering*) Come out here. (*She grabs the cane again*)

Billy winces, then quickly stuffs some books down his trousers to protect his bottom. He then moves out and bends down with a smile

(*Crossly*) Oh, stand up.

Surprised, Billy stands

Put your hand out.
Billy Eh?
Mother Goose Put your hand out.

Billy winces and cautiously holds his hand out palm up

Take that. (*She hits his palm with the cane*)
Billy Owwwwwww. (*He sticks his hand under his armpit*)
Mother Goose Now get back to your seat and stop showing off. Do you think you're the teacher in this class, or something? (*She puts the cane down*)
Billy No, mum.
Mother Goose Then stop acting like a brainless idiot. (*She realizes what she has said and reacts*) I think we'd better forget about maths. We'll do some Geography instead.

Billy moves back to his seat

All groan at the announcement

Mother Goose (*cleaning the blackboard*) Now then ... who can tell me where the Andes are?
Sage On the end of the wristies. (*He dangles his hands limply*)

All laugh

Clarence enters R

Clarence And what is the meaning of all this levity?

Mother Goose They saw your face as the door opened. What are you doing here in my school? Go away and mind your own business.

Clarence (*smirking*) But this *is* my business. As Squire of the village, I am the official Inspector of Schools, and unless I'm satisfied with the standards of your teaching, I can close the whole place down. Understand?

Mother Goose Ooo-er.

Clarence (*looking round the class*) Now then . . . is there anything remarkable about any of these pupils?

Mother Goose Well . . . two of them have got good manners.

Clarence (*pointing at Sage*) You, boy. Where are the Kings and Queens of England usually crowned?

Sage (*standing smartly*) Er . . . on the head.

All cheer and applaud

Clarence Bah. (*To Onions*) You there. What is a comet?

Onions A small star with a tail on it. (*He stands*)

The seat tips and Billy is thrown to the floor

All laugh

Billy scrabbles about and rights the bench

Clarence (*glaring at him*) You there . . . Assuming I accept that a comet is a small star with a tail on it . . . can you give me the *name* of one?

Billy Er . . . er . . . Lassie.

All laugh

Clarence fumes

Clarence (*firmly*) What name do we give to the outer part of a tree?

No one answers

(*Angrily*) Bark, you fools. Bark.

All Woof, woof.

Clarence (*glaring at Mother Goose*) Bah. It's perfectly obvious to me that you, madam, are the most incompetent teacher I've ever come across. These students of yours know nothing. It gives me great pleasure to close this school down.

Mother Goose (*stricken*) Oh, no. You can't. Not my little school.

Billy (*jumping up*) Oooh, you rotten spiteful old skinflint. You're only doing this because you're jealous of my mum. (*To the audience*) Isn't he, kids?

Audience and school reaction

Clarence (*caught out*) Nonsense. Ridiculous. My decision is based entirely on my vast knowledge of things. And just to prove it . . . if anyone can ask *me* a question I can't answer, I'll change my mind and allow the place to stay open. (*He adopts a smug attitude*)

Sage (*To Onions*) Here ... now's your chance. We can find out how much we're going to get paid for working for him this past twelve months.

Onions How?

Sage Listen to this. (*He stands*) Please, Squire. (*He puts his hand up*)

Clarence (*grandly*) Yes?

Sage If two men work for a year, and get paid two pounds an hour ... how much money will they have when they finally get their wages?

Clarence Simple. They won't have anything.

Onions (*jumping up*) How do you work *that* out?

Billy quickly reverses the bench and sits

Clarence It's easy. (*He crosses to the blackboard and picks up the chalk*) There are three hundred and sixty-five days in a year. Correct?

Mother Goose Except in Leap Year, when there's three hundred and sixty-six.

Clarence Very well. (*He writes three hundred and sixty-six on the board*) Now assuming they work eight hours a day ... and there are twenty-four hours in a day ... they only work a third of a day. Correct?

Sage
Onions } (*together*) Yes.

Clarence And three into three hundred and sixty-six equals one hundred and twenty-two, doesn't it? (*He writes it down*) Now they don't work either Saturday or Sunday, do they?

Sage
Onions } (*together*) Well ... no.

Clarence And there are fifty-two Saturdays and fifty-two Sundays in each year ... which means one hundred and four days they don't work anyway ... and one hundred and four from one hundred and twenty-two leaves eighteen, doesn't it? (*He writes it down*)

Sage
Onions } (*together*) Well, yes ... but ... but ...

Clarence And we mustn't forget they have *two weeks holiday*, must we? So deduct fourteen days from eighteen, and we have only four remaining.

Sage
Onions } (*miserably*) Four days pay.

Clarence Not at all ... there are also the four Public *Bank Holidays* ... and four from four equals *nothing*.

Sage So we're sunk.

Onions We don't get a penny.

Clarence No ... but *I* do. As this *isn't* a Leap year, you owe me eight hours work and eight hours at two pounds an hour equals sixteen pounds. You owe me sixteen pounds each. (*Loudly*) Class dismissed.

Clarence exits R

The classroom breaks into an uproar. Billy jumps up. Sage and Onions reverse the bench quickly. Billy sits and is tipped onto the floor. The scene ends in chaos

The Lights fade to Black-out

SCENE 4

A Quiet Street

Harmony enters R with a smile

Harmony   Poor Mother Goose, once more it seems her plans have gone
awry.
But never fear, her star grows bright to dominate the sky.
The eggs of gold and her kind heart have comfort brought to
many.
Her wealth is shared by ev'ryone ...

Discord enters L

Discord   She grudges ev'ry penny.
Beneath that simp'ring, wrinkled face: those clothes of silk
and gold.
Her mind is dark and greedy and her heart is hard and cold.
Just mark my words, within a week you'll see her colours true;
And then, my friend, the game is mine ... and Fairy land's
crown too.

Harmony   I somehow doubt that statement, for there's something you
forget.
The magic goose, Priscilla, can outwit you even yet.
As long as *she* is close at hand your powers have no strength.
So plot and plan, dear Discord. We'll meet again ... at length.

Harmony exits R

Discord (*fuming*) Botheration. For once that meddlesome creature is right.
I have to get rid of that goose before she ruins my plan. (*She chuckles*)
Aha ... I have it. Everything is falling into place ... just as I want it to.
(*She gives a nasty laugh*)

Discord exits L

As she does so, the Lights brighten

Jill and Colin enter R, looking very happy

Jill Oh, I'm absolutely exhausted. We've delivered invitations to all the
nobility for miles around.

Colin And if everyone turns up, it'll be the biggest party of all time. I can't
believe how much it's costing.

Jill Thanks to darling Priscilla, we don't have to worry about *that*. Every
morning for the past two weeks she's laid another golden egg. Oh, Colin.
We must be the luckiest people in the world.

Colin And the richest, I shouldn't wonder. Uncle Clarence is green with envy. He's desperately trying to think of some way to get his hands on part of the money at least.

Jill I know. He even offered mother fifty pounds to let him buy Priscilla. (*She laughs*)

Colin I can't wait to see his face when he sees your new home. It's the grandest place in the whole county.

Jill It'll be even grander by tomorrow. Mother's having the place redecorated for the party. By the time it's finished, it'll look like a palace.

Colin And so it should. Where else would a Princess like you live?

Jill (*laughing*) I'm not a Princess.

Colin You are to me.

Jill Then I'm a very poor sort of Princess. I don't even know how to dance.

Colin (*with amusement*) You don't? But Jill ... everybody can dance.

Jill Not me. Tomorrow night I'll just have to sit there and watch the others.

Colin Not if I've anything to do with it. Jill Goose, you're about to have your first dancing lesson, and by tomorrow night you'll be the belle of the ball.

Jill and Colin sing and dance

Song 6 and Dance

At the end of the song they exit L

Mother Goose enters R *in a fantastic, hideous gown*

Mother Goose (*beaming*) Do you like the frock? (*She displays it*) It's called the "Racing car" look. (*She smooths her bust*) Hugs tightly round the curves. I bought it in (*she names a local shop*). Got it for a ridiculous figure. Oh, and then I popped down the road for a pair of shoes. I found a marvellous pair in a lovely shade of Puce Magenta with delirium trimmings and crepe soles, but when I tried them on ... ooh, the agony. I said to the assistant, "Here ... these shoes are too tight. I'll never be able to walk in 'em," and she looked at me as though I were a dirty shirt and she were a packet of Persil, and said "Modom ... people who buy shoes in *our* shop don't have to walk.

Clarence enters R

Clarence (*aside*) That old idiot, Mother Goose ... and all alone. Now's my chance to make up to her and get these eager little fingers into that mountain of gold she owns. (*Aloud*) Ahem ... If it isn't the lovely Madam de Goosey. (*He shows his teeth in a forced smile*)

Mother Goose Hallo ... I didn't know they'd re-released *Jaws*.

Clarence (*crossing to her*) I can't tell you how pleased I am to see you.

Mother Goose (*flirting*) Oh ... I wish I could say the same. (*She preens her hair*)

Clarence (*aside*) She could if she lied as well as *I* do. (*Aloud*) I passed your new house this morning.

Mother Goose How very kind of you.

Clarence (*sniffing*) Hmmmmm. What is that lovely perfume you're wearing? Pink Gardenia at five thousand pounds a gramme?

Mother Goose No. Pink paraffin at ninety pence a litre.

Clarence (*passionately*) Oh, Benzedrine . . .

Mother Goose Clementine.

Clarence Oh. I *do* beg your pardon. Oh, Clementine . . . grant me the favour of one little kiss from those ruby red lips of yours.

Mother Goose No, I don't think so. I have got scruples, you know.

Clarence That's all right. I've been vaccinated. (*Passionately*) Ahhhh, my beloved. Such is your fascination, I can hardly restrain myself from smothering you with kisses.

Mother Goose (*to the audience*) Just think . . . and it's only two weeks since he'd have been trying to do it with a cushion.

Clarence (*flinging himself on one knee*) Marry me.

Mother Goose Oh, go on. You don't mean it. (*Hopefully*) Do you?

Clarence I do. I do. (*Aside to the audience*) There's no depths I wouldn't sink to for money.

Mother Goose (*weakening*) Well . . .

Clarence (*begging*) Please. Please.

Mother Goose (*making her mind up*) No. I couldn't possibly marry you just yet. I mean . . . we hardly know each other. Here . . . I'll tell you what, though. I'm throwing a party at Goose Grange tomorrow night. How would you like to come to that?

Clarence (*standing*) Oh, Turpentine . . .

Mother Goose Clementine. (*Brightly*) I've invited everybody of any importance, but I'm sure nobody will mind if *you* turn up as well.

Clarence Oh . . . well . . . I'd be delighted.

Mother Goose Just press the doorbell with your nose and somebody will let you in.

Clarence With my *nose*?

Mother Goose Well, you won't be coming empty-handed, will you? (*Excitedly*) Oh, there'll be all sorts of fabulous foods, bottles of champagne and barrels and barrels of rabbit beer.

Clarence (*blankly*) Rabbit beer? What's that?

Mother Goose It's the same as ordinary beer but it's got more hops in it. Here . . . and you can dance, can't you, 'cos there's going to be lots of dancing.

Clarence Me? Dance? (*Smugly*) My dear Mother Goose. I used to be a professional tap dancer. Had to give it up though. Kept falling into the sink. (*He offers his arm*) Allow me to walk you home.

Mother Goose (*taking it*) You can say what you like, girls. This is one man who knows what to give the girl who's got everything. *Encouragement.*

Mother Goose and Clarence exit R

The Lights fade to Black-out

SCENE 5

The Ballroom of Goose Grange

When the scene begins, Villagers in their finery (or fancy dress) are singing and dancing. Footmen carry trays of drinks around the room and a party atmosphere prevails

Song 7

At the end of the song, everyone falls back, dividing themselves into groups at the outer edges of the ballroom. They chat animatedly but silently and sip their champagne

Sage and Onions enter UR, *wearing "posh" outfits. They move* DS

Sage Cor, what a smashing party. I've never eaten so much in all my life.
Onions Me neither. Here . . . what did you think to those new vegetables? The ones that were a cross between a potato and a bath sponge.
Sage Oooh, they were terrible. Mind you, they did hold a lot of gravy. No, my favourite was the trifle. Yum, yum. (*He smacks his lips*)
Onions Yes, I liked that as well . . . except for one thing. I found a feather in the custard.
Sage Well what did you expect? It was *Birds*.

Jill enters UR *in a very pretty gown*

Jill (*brightly*) Everyone to the Terrace room, please. There's a gold egg for every guest, so don't be late.

With cries of delight everyone hurries off L

As soon as they have gone, Jill buries her head in her hands and begins to cry

Colin enters UR

Colin (*with concern*) Jill. What's the matter? (*He hurries to her*)
Jill Oh, Colin, I'm so unhappy. I thought that when mother became rich, everything would be wonderful . . . but it *isn't*. We invited every Lord and Lady in the county to tonight's party, but not one of them's turned up. She's going to be *so* hurt.
Colin Don't be upset, Jill. I'm sure they'll be along soon. Society people are *always* late. Besides . . . who could resist accepting your invitation? Mother Goose is the wealthiest woman in the land and the food in the banqueting hall is incredible.
Jill That's just the trouble. They're so jealous of her new-found riches, they've decided to ignore her. I'm sure of it. That dreadful uncle of yours is the only one who came, which is why I had to hurry round and invite the Villagers along. (*Sadly*) How on earth are we going to tell her? She's so excited about everything.
Colin Cheer up. I'm sure everything's going to be all right. Besides . . . I can't bear to see you looking so sad. Come on. Give me a smile. Please.

Jill gives a wan smile

That's better. Now come on. Let's go see if any of the nobility are arriving.

Colin and Jill exit DR

As they do so, the Lights dim

Discord enters UL. *She moves* DCF

Discord (*sneering*) You'll watch in vain, you little fools. With the aid of my magic powers, I've made quite sure that tonight's celebration will be for my benefit only.
(*Sarcastically*)   Poor Mother Gose,
                        In ballroom bright,
                        Your downfall comes,
                        This very night.

Priscilla enters UR, *behind Discord*

                        Disaster, I, Discord induce.
                        (*She turns and sees Priscilla*)
                        Confound it. It's the magic goose.

Priscilla scrapes the floor with one foot in a menacing attitude

(*Backing away*) Nice goose . . . pretty Priscilla.

Priscilla advances on her with determination

(*Backing further*) Get away, you stupid bird. Leave me alone.

Priscilla runs at her

With a scream of terror Discord takes to her heels and exits

Lights up

Priscilla does a little victory dance, then suddenly catches sight of the Teddy. She moves towards it

Audience reaction

Billy enters in his party suit

Billy Take your hands off my Teddy . . . oh . . . it's *you* Priscilla. Here . . . what are *you* doing inside the house? You've got a beautiful big house all of your own, now, you know.

Priscilla whispers in his ear

It's lonely out there? Yes, I suppose it is. I expect all your servants are in here enjoying themselves, aren't they?

Priscilla nods

And you've got nobody to talk to

Priscilla shakes her head

No. I'm a bit like that as well. Except for you and Mum and Jill and

Colin, not many people speak to me. I suppose it's because I'm daft, isn't it?

Priscilla shakes her head

Yes, it is. I'm just the village idiot.

Priscilla shakes her head

Yes, I am.

Priscilla shakes her head

Yes, I am.

Priscilla does nothing

(*Nudging her*) Hey ... that's your cue. You're supposed to shake your head.

Priscilla still does nothing

(*Peering under her*) Is anybody in there? Come on. Tell me I'm not.

Priscilla shakes her head

(*Laughing*) Oh, you were pulling my leg, weren't you?

Priscilla nods

Here ... I'll tell you what. I'll nip out and get us some drinks and sandwiches, and we'll have a little party all on our own, eh? How would you like that?

Priscilla nods, then whispers in his ear

What kind of sandwiches? Well ... what kind would you like? Pâté?

Priscilla quickly backs away

Ooops, sorry. Here ... look. Let's forget about the sandwiches. We'll just stay here and have a little chat, shall we? 'Cos I'd sooner be with you than anybody else in the world. (*He puts his arm round Priscilla and sings*)

Song 8

At the end of the song, Mother Goose enters UR, *in a dazzling, outrageous costume with a very low neckline*

Mother Goose Do you like it girls? (*She parades it*) It's my religious dress. Lo and Behold.

Billy Oh, Mum ... you look just like a film star.

Mother Goose (*preening*) Greta Garbo?

Billy No. ET. (*He laughs*) Here ... do you know ET never got home.

Mother Goose No, I didn't. What happened?

Billy He was attacked by a Zanussi washing machine.

Mother Goose Listen, you ... (*she sees Priscilla*) What's Priscilla doing in here? She should be tucked up in her little four poster.

Billy She's come to the party.

Mother Goose We can't have geese running about the place all night. Somebody might tread on her. Besides . . . she's leaving straw all over the carpet. Take her back to her little house and lock her in for the night. We don't want anybody to run off with her, do we?
Billy But, Mum . . .
Mother Goose Don't argue. Do as you're told. Now . . . (*she looks round*) Where's all me guests gone?
Billy (*sadly*) Come on, Priscilla. (*He leads Priscilla* UR)

Clarence enters DL

Billy and Priscilla come to a halt upstage and listen

Clarence (*with false pleasure*) Ah, my dear Vaseline.
Mother Goose Clementine. (*Gushingly*) So pleased you could come. What do you think to the old place?
Clarence (*airily*) Well . . . I suppose it's quite attractive if you like this sort of thing. But why don't you have a large chandelier?
Mother Goose Well, I did think about it, but no one in our family can play one. (*She looks off* R) Oh, do excuse me. There's someone else. (*She crosses him to greet Jill and Colin*)

Jill and Colin enter DR

Welcome to Goose Grange. (*She recognizes Colin and reacts*) Oh . . . what's Colin doing here? I didn't invite *him*.
Jill No. But *I* did.
Mother Goose But he's poor. I've only invited rich people. I want to impress them, you see. I'm ever so sorry, Colin, but you'll have to go. You can stand in the garden and watch them arrive, if you like.
Colin (*gently*) I'm sorry, too, Mother Goose . . . but there won't be any rich people coming. They've all returned their invitations. We're the only ones here.

The Villagers begin to re-enter casually

Mother Goose (*stricken*) You mean . . . just *us* . . . and these village people? (*She looks around them, brokenly*) And I thought it was going to be such a wonderful party. (*She sniffles and dabs at her eyes*)
Billy (*coming downstage*) But it *will* be, Mum. We've got the food . . . we've got the music . . . and most of all we've got our *friends*. It's going to be the party of a lifetime.

All agree

Mother Goose (*brightening*) Yes, you're right. I don't know what I was thinking of. The money must have gone to my head for the minute. Who cares about them stuck-up snobs? I'm surrounded by friends and you're all very welcome. So if everybody's here that's coming, we may as well enjoy ourselves. Let's have a "knees-up". Come on, everybody. Take your partners for the "Giddy Goose Hoe-down".

Everyone but Clarence cheers and with whoops and yells form themselves into a hoe-down team and explode into action. Even Priscilla joins in

Clarence retreats to the side of the ballroom and watches in horror as the dancers whirl

Song 9—The Hoe Down

At the end of the song all cheer loudly

Clarence (*with disgust*) Bah . . . this entire party is a fiasco. Not an ounce of breeding or good manners anywhere. It's no wonder that none of my rich friends came along. You're a disgrace to the neighbourhood.

Billy Into the moat with him. Chuck him into the water.

All cheer loudly

Clarence gives a yell of fear and races off with everyone but Mother Goose following him

Mother Goose Oh, well . . . I suppose that's put an end to me party. (*She yawns*) Oooh, I do feel tired. Must be all the excitement. I could sleep for a hundred years. (*She totters forwards* DC) Perhaps I'll dream of a fairy prince coming to wake me up again? (*She yawns*) Mind you . . . if he's a fairy, I don't suppose there'll be much doing. (*She yawns again*)

Unnoticed by her. Discord enters UL *and casts magical spells at her*

The Lights dim

Mother Goose's eyes close

Discord   In slumber deep she'll gently rest, and soon you'll see who comes off best.

With something gold can never buy, to tempt old Mother Goose I'll try.

I'll make her sorry with her lot; she'll *crave* for what she hasn't got.

Forsaking both her friends and duty to search in vain for youth and beauty.

She laughs harshly and signals

A large mirror in an ornate frame is carried on by two muscular men in green body make-up and tattered chiffon drapery. They carry it USC. *The whole effect should be one of evil*

Discord gestures

Mother Goose opens her eyes sleepily

Mother Goose (*dazedly*) Oh . . . I must have dropped off. Mind you, I'm not surprised. It's gone a bit gloomy in here. I think the candles must have burned away. I *was* going to have electric lights fitted, but I changed my mind after trying one. I was up half the night trying to blow it out. (*She turns and sees Discord*) Oh . . . who are you?

Discord A friend. (*She moves closer*) Come to prove that though you're blessed with gold, your wealth is but a jest.

Mother Goose A jest? How can it be? I've got everything a woman could wish for.

Discord Indeed? Then in this frame now cast an eye ... (*she indicates the mirror*) Your future in its depths could lie.

Mother Goose (*eyeing the men*) I like the supporting pieces. (*She peers into the mirror*) Good heavens. What a dreadful-looking mess. I suppose this is what you call Modern Art, is it?

Discord No. It's what I call a mirror.

Mother Goose Eh? (*She looks again*) Oh ... it's true. And that ugly old woman inside it ... it's *me*. (*She turns away covering her face*) Take it away. Take it away.

Discord First look again and you will see yourself as you would *wish* to be.

Mother Goose reluctantly turns and looks again

Mother Goose Ohhhhhh. I'm beautiful. Beautiful. (*She admires herself*)

Discord Oh, no. Not yet. You haven't paid the price.
You have your wealth ... let *that* suffice.

Mother Goose (*turning to her*) I'll give it up. You can have every penny. Just let me be young and beautiful as I am in the mirror. Please. (*She drops to her knees*)

Discord (*smirking*) For beauty, on her knees she begs.
(*To Mother Goose*) Will you give up the golden eggs?
Renounce your friends and family
And ever be a slave to *me*?

Mother Goose Anything. Anything.

Discord (*triumphantly*) And should I bid you form a noose
To strangle that accursed goose?

Mother Goose (*startled*) Priscilla? Harm Priscilla?

Discord Well? Well?

Mother Goose (*jumping up*) No, no. Never. Not even for beauty. Go away. I never want to see you again.

Mother Goose hurries off UR

Discord gives a shriek of laughter

Discord In vain she runs. The seed is sown
And very soon her soul I'll own.
From henceforth Mother Goose will dream
Of youthful figure ... skin of cream.
Golden hair and perfect face.
And then will come her fall from grace.
(*She laughs again and signals*)

The two men remove the mirror

As they do so, Harmony enters in a white spotlight

Discord moves back

Harmony You'll find you've got a lot to learn
If that is your intention.
The victory you claim, I fear

Is nothing but invention.
Dear Mother Goose will cast aside
Whate'er temptations *you* provide,
And though you strive with all your might,
She'll foil your plan and win the fight.

Discord   We'll see. No solace will she find in eggs of shining gold,
If all remind her constantly her face is worn and old.
In torment she'll return to me to beg for features fair.
And then for me ... the Fairy Crown. For Mother
Goose ... despair.

Discord gives a harsh laugh and exits DL

Harmony   Fear not. For with Priscilla's aid,
My *own* plans have been duly laid;
And Mother Goose shall win the day
If truth and goodness here hold sway.
So here tonight, in peace she'll sleep
Whilst fairies, guardian watch shall keep.
We'll fill her dreams with sweet content
Until the dark of night is spent.
(*She waves her wand*)

The Lights brighten

Fairies carrying flower garlands flow onto the stage in graceful attitudes

A ballet commences in which Harmony becomes the central character and, if possible, glittering gauzes drop in from above, each decorated with flowers. By the end of the ballet the room resembles a great Floral Hall. Fairies should be in tableaux with flowers forming a central arch. It is important, and for best theatrical impact, that a colour co-ordination is made for this scene. I suggest white, pink and possibly pale blue

10—Ballet

Fairies in tableaux

Mother Goose, Priscilla and other principals if required, enter through the arch and assemble C. *As the music ends, they take their applause*

The CURTAIN *falls but should rise almost at once for a Tableaux Finish*

Segue the ballet music until the end of the second CURTAIN *fall*

The CURTAIN *falls*

ACT II

SCENE 1

The Grounds of Goose Grange

A large garden with graceful weeping willows, fountains and a huge glazed conservatory in the background. UC *is an old statue of a nymph, face partially chipped away and in a poor state of repair. Rosewalks and floral bowers flank the wing spaces. A white garden seat is down* L

When the scene begins, it is daylight and the Villagers in finery are parading about the gardens and admiring the views. As they do so, they sing happily and a group of dancers perform a spirited dance

Song 11

At the end of the song, Sage and Onions enter UL. *They are dressed as footmen and carry themselves grandly*

Sage Ladies and Gentiles.

Onions Crocodiles and Reptiles.

Sage ⎫
Onions ⎭ (*together*) Refreshments are now being served.

With delight, the Villagers exit L

Sage (*relaxing*) Cor. This is the life. I'd much rather be a footman for Mother Goose than I would a bailiff for Creepy Clarence.

Onions Same here. At least we get paid every week and we're never short of food. Here ... I wonder how the *new* bailiff's getting on?

Sage Oh, haven't you heard? The police picked him up for shoplifting last week. He pinched ten metres of elastic.

Onions And what happened?

Sage He went to gaol for a long stretch.

Onions I nearly went to gaol once, you know. For trying to drive a donkey cart under a low bridge.

Sage Eh?

Onions Well, I was driving along this dirt-track when we came to a bridge and the donkey couldn't get under it. So I got my hammer and chisel out and started chipping away at the brickwork. All of a sudden, this big daft policeman came up and asked me what I was doing, so I had to tell him.

Sage And what did he say?

Onions He told me I was daft. I should have dug part of the dirt-track up instead of damaging the bridge, but it was *him* that was the daft one. I mean ... it was the donkey's *ears* that were too long ... not his legs.

Sage (*wincing*) I suppose you know a lot about animals, don't you?

Onions Oh, yes.

Sage Well in that case, you can give me a bit of advice. I've lost my little dog and can't find him anywhere. What do you think I should do about it?

Onions Why don't you put an advert in the papers?

Sage How will that help? He can't read.

Onions Well . . . what's his name?

Sage Carpenter.

Onions Carpenter? That's a funny name for a dog.

Sage No it isn't. He does little jobs round the house.

Clarence enters UR *furtively*

Clarence (*in a hoarse whisper*) Ah . . . the very men I'm looking for. I've got a job for you.

Sage Sorry, Squire. We're not working for you any more. Remember?

Clarence Not even if I increase the wages you're getting from Mother Goose?

Onions Don't be daft. We get a golden egg each week.

Clarence And if I were to give you *two* golden eggs each week?

Sage
Onions } (*together*) What do we have to do?

Clarence (*smiling in triumph*) That's better. Draw closer and I'll explain.

They quickly flank the Squire

As Squire of Merrilea, the magic goose should rightfully be *mine*. After all . . . it *was* wandering round on *my* property. That being the case, it was stolen from me by Mother Goose and I intend to get it back. I'll keep her occupied whilst you two snatch it from the stables and take it to Cheatem Hall. Lock it in the cellar and wait for my return. And remember . . . let no one near her till I arrive. Understand?

Sage
Onions } (*together*) Roger and out.

Clarence Off you go then. I can see the decrepit old harridan heading this way.

Sage and Onions quickly exit DL

Mother Goose enters UR *in her finery. She sees Clarence and reacts*

Mother Goose Good Heavens. Who left that scarecrow in my garden?

Clarence (*gushingly*) Ah, my dear Mother Goose . . . Margarine.

Mother Goose *Clementine* (*Frostily*) How dare you protrude into my private undergrowth? Leave the vicinity at once.

Clarence But I've come to beg your forgiveness, my angel.

Mother Goose (*startled*) Eh? (*She recovers herself*) Oh, no you don't. You're not going to pull the wool over *my* thighs. Never dorken my darkstep again.

Clarence Ah, my sweet one. My behaviour last week was inexcusable. How can I make amends?

Mother Goose (*weakening*) Well . . . I might forgive you if you helped me out with a bit of social ettiquetti.

Clarence Your wish is my command. Let's sit upon this bench and you can tell me your problem.

He takes her arm and they sit on the bench

Mother Goose Well . . . now that I'm rich and famous, I want to meet other famous ladies.

Clarence Ah . . . like (*He names several well-known nobility*) and the Duchess, for instance?

Mother Goose (*blankly*) Eh?

Clarence You . . . er . . . you *do* know what a Duchess *is*, don't you?

Mother Goose Of course I do. It's the same as an English S.

Clarence winces

Anyway . . . I thought it might be nice to start a Club, and what I want to know *is* . . . Do you think there *should* be Clubs for women like me?

Clarence Oh, *yes*. (*Aside*) Big heavy ones.

Mother Goose (*happily*) There . . . I knew I could rely on *you*. (*Suddenly*) Here . . . there's just one other thing I want to get sorted out, though. I've heard rumours that you've been telling everyone in the village that I'm a flea-bitten, addle-pated, knock-kneed, cross-eyed nincompoop.

Clarence (*indignantly*) I certainly haven't. I didn't even know you were knock-kneed.

Mother Goose Oh, well that's all right, then. And now we've settled that, we can get down to discussing our wedding plans, can't we? (*She simpers*)

Clarence (*startled*) Eh?

Mother Goose Well . . . you did say last week you wanted me to be your awful wedded wife.

Clarence I *did*?

Mother Goose There. I knew you'd remember. (*She beams*) Oh, what a surprise you're going to get when you see me in my wedding dress. I shall be all pink and dimpled.

Clarence (*aside*) She means all drink and pimpled. (*He rises*) I'm terribly sorry, Tangerine . . .

Mother Goose *Clementine*.

Clarence But a marriage between *us* is totally out of the question. You're far too ugly to marry a member of the upper classes.

Mother Goose Eh?

Clarence (*proudly*) After all . . . *my* ancestors sprang from a long line of Peers.

Mother Goose (*jumping up*) Yes . . . six of them jumped off the docks. (*With annoyance*) Now listen here, you stuck-up stick of salami sausage . . .

Clarence (*with outrage*) Stuck-up? Me?

Mother Goose Yes. You. Your nose is so far up in the air, every time you sneeze you blow your hat off. If you refuse to marry me, I shall sue you.

Clarence On *what* grounds, may I ask?

Mother Goose On the recreation grounds.

Clarence Bah. (*He turns away*) Au revoir. (*Contemptuously*) That's goodbye in French.

Mother Goose Oh, is it? Well *Cyanide* to you, mate. That's goodbye in *any* language.

Clarence Hah.

Clarence exits DL

Mother Goose Oh, I've been jilted. (*She sobs loudly*)

Jill and Colin enter UR

Colin Mother Goose.

Jill Mother. (*She hurries to her*) What's wrong?

Mother Goose (*sniffling*) Oh, it's nothing. I'm just letting me emulsions get the better of me. All this money and nobody to share it with. (*She sighs*)

Jill But you're sharing it with *everyone*. The village hasn't been so happy in years.

Mother Goose I don't mean *that* kind of sharing. I mean I've got nobody special. You've got Colin and Billy's got his Teddy bear ... but *me* ... I've got nobody. (*She sniffles again*)

Colin (*gently*) You've got Priscilla.

Mother Goose (*helplessly*) Yes, I know ... and she's the most beautiful goose in the world. But what I *really* want is to get married again.

Jill Married?

Mother Goose I thought now I was rich, I'd have hundreds of men at my feet ... but the only one who's been near 'em lately, is my chiropodist. (*She sighs*)

Colin What kind of husband are you looking for?

Mother Goose A live one.

Colin No. I mean ... what are you looking for most? Charm ... wealth ... or appearance?

Mother Goose Appearance. And the sooner the better. I mean ... I'm not asking for much, am I? Just a man like my first husband. One who wouldn't argue with me.

Jill Didn't you ever argue with father?

Mother Goose No. Oh, we sometimes had a few words in bed, but we never fell out. (*She sighs deeply*) I suppose I'd better go see if everybody's enjoying themselves.

Mother Goose exits L *in a very dejected manner*

Jill (*watching her go*) Poor mother. I didn't realize she was so unhappy.

Colin She hasn't been the same person since the night of the Ball.

Jill If only there were something we could do to cheer her up.

Colin (*looking round*) The garden's looking a bit overgrown. Perhaps she might feel better if we tidied things up.

Jill Yes. (*She looks at the statue*) Perhaps we could do something with *her*?

Colin (*turning to look at it*) Hmm. Her face is a bit off-putting.

Mother Goose re-enters in time to hear the remark

Jill I'm afraid so. She's not very attractive at all.

Mother Goose reacts

Colin I think she needs some sort of restoration work done on her to cover the cracks. Perhaps a coat of sand and cement.

Mother Goose reacts again

Jill It might help if her nose were shortened, too. And straightened.

Mother Goose reacts again and exits DL

(*Turning to face front again*) All the same . . . I'm sure everything's going to be perfect when the workmen have finished. Aren't you?

Colin It's all perfect now . . . at least for *me*. You're beside me. Our wedding day is fixed for next month and from now on we're going to live happily ever after.

Colin and Jill sing a duet

Song 12

After the song, they exit UR

Mother Goose enters DL

Mother Goose (*upset*) I wouldn't have believed it if I hadn't seen it with my own lips. My own daughter. Casting nasturtiums on my cabbages. Thank goodness I've still got my little Billy. He'll never turn against me.

Billy enters UR

Billy Hi, Mum.

Mother Goose Yes. It's the slope in the lawn. (*Stricken*) Oh, Billy . . . my little baby boy. Come to your poor old mother. (*She holds her arms out to him*) Your poor unwanted mother. (*She sobs*)

Billy (*blankly*) Eh? What's wrong?

Mother Goose I'll tell you what's wrong. It's that Colin and your little sister Jill. All the time they've been patting me on the back, they were just looking for the best place to stick a knife in it. Ohhhhh. And when I think of all the things I've done for them.

Billy I don't know what you're talking about.

Mother Goose No, but you're going to find out. I'm going to leave you every penny in my Will when I get ready to make it out. That'll teach 'em a lesson.

Billy Oh, well in that case, can you lend me a pound now. I want to buy some sweets and a comic.

Mother Goose Lend you a pound? Certainly not. My mother never let *me* spend money on sweets and comics.

Billy Oooh, you must have had a rotten mother, then.

Mother Goose (*with annoyance*) I'd a better mother than *you've* got.

Billy Oh, come on, Mum. Lend me a pound.

Mother Goose (*crossly*) No. You're not having a penny. From now on, nobody is having anything from me. (*She turns away*)

Billy Oh, you bad-tempered old woman. (*He pulls a face at her back*)

Mother Goose (*spinning to face him*) You've just pulled a face at me, haven't you?

Billy No, I haven't.

Mother Goose Yes, you have. I heard the audience laughing. Well let me tell you this, Billy Goose ... It's neither funny not clever to make ugly faces. Anybody can do it. *I* can make uglier faces than *you* any day of the week.

Billy I'm not surprised. You've got a head start. You're ugly already.

Mother Goose (*indignantly*) You're drunk.

Billy Maybe ... but in the morning *I'll* be sober.

Mother Goose Oooh, you little monster. (*She slaps him*)

Billy (*howling*) Owwww. You've shattered me concentration. (*He clutches his arm*) You're a nasty, horrible, ugly old woman, and I never want to speak to you again.

Billy runs off DR *crying*

Mother Goose (*striken*) Billy ... come back. Too late. He's gone. (*Dazed*) What's wrong with me? Why is everybody turning against me? I've tried to make them all happy but nobody seems to want me any more. The Squire won't marry me. Colin and Jill want to cover me in cement and Billy never wants to speak to me again. And I thought they had problems in *East Enders*. (*She sobs*)

Discord enters DL

The Lights dim

Discord (*aside*)   Success is near. Now watch this
Prime example of humanity
Fall straight into temptation's arms
To satisfy her vanity.
(*Aloud to Mother Goose*)
Oh, foolish woman, can't you see
You're old and ugly as can be,
And ev'ryone despises you. Admit it.

Mother Goose Yes. It's true. It's true.

Discord   If you were beautiful as me, how differently things would be.
The world would call itself your friend, and happiness would never end.
But if my face resembled yours and no young man would pat it.
I'd stick it on the garden wall, and throw a breeze block at it.

Mother Goose buries her face in her hands

    But never fear. If you will pay the meagre price I ask,
Eternal beauty shall be yours; in perfect bliss you'll bask.

Mother Goose (*eagerly*) What is it? What do you want from me?

Discord (*harshly*) The magic goose ... *Priscilla*.

Mother Goose (*horrified*) No. No. Anything but her.

Discord   Then fare you well. In ugliness you'll live throughout
                              your life.

                              You'll have no *friends*. No *family* . . . and never be a *wife*.
                              (*She turns as though to exit*)

Mother Goose (*desperately*) Wait. (*Sadly*) If you promise you'll take good
care of her . . . I'll do it. You can have her.

Discord laughs in triumph

Harmony enters DR

Harmony   (*to Mother Goose*) One moment. Lend an ear to reason.
                              Discord leads you into treason.

Mother Goose (*indignantly*) I beg your pardon? I don't know what this has
got to do with you, young woman, but what I do with my own goose is
entirely my own affair. Mind your own business. I'm going to be made
young and beautiful (*To Discord*) Lead on. Take me to your beauty
parlour.

Harmony   (*insistently*) You're almost lost. Resist her spells.
                              Ignore the tempting tale she tells.
                              Don't search for beauty. Be content
                              I *beg* of you . . . or you'll repent.

Mother Goose (*tartly*) Oh, I know what your trouble is. You're scared I'm
going to look prettier than you, aren't you? Well you're dead right. I'm
going to be the prettiest woman in the entire world. (*To Discord*) Which
way do we go?

Discord smirks and indicates DL

Mother Goose sneers at Harmony and exits DL *in a hurry*

Discord   (*delightedly*) Her discontent is openly confessed.
                              She rushes to destruction like the rest.

She gives a mocking bow to Harmony and follows Mother Goose off

Harmony   (*sadly*) As Goodness, Mother Goose has spurned,
                              Priscilla now must be returned
                              To Fairyland . . . where we in sorrow
                              Greet Queen Discord on the morrow.

The Lights quickly fade to Black-out

SCENE 2

Outside Cheatem Hall

Sage and Onions enter L *leading Priscilla by means of a rope tied about her
neck. They move* C

Sage (*with relief*) Phew . . . we made it. You don't think anyone saw us, do
you?

Onions Course they didn't. All we've got to do now is to get her into the

Squire's cellar and Bob's your uncle. (*He tugs on the rope*) Come on, goosie.

Priscilla shakes her head

Sage Here ... I don't think she wants to come.
Onions Yes she does. (*To Priscilla*) Don't you?

Priscilla shakes her head

Oh, yes you do.
Sage Oh, no she doesn't.
Onions Oh, yes she does.

Audience reaction

Well you're going to go whether you like it or not. Get behind her, Sage, and we'll *push* her into the Hall

Sage goes behind Priscilla who promptly sits

Sage Ooh. She's suddenly sat sitted. Now what are we going to do?
Onions Don't panic. I'll think of something. I'm not the son of a famous inventor for nothing, you know.
Sage (*with surprise*) You're the son of a famous inventor? Who was that?
Onions My dad, of course. The most famous inventor ever to set foot out of Ireland.
Sage *I've* never heard of an Irish inventor.
Onions Course you have. You must have seen his name on hundreds of things he invented.
Sage What is it?
Onions Pat Pending.
Sage Cor ... he must have been a very rich man.
Onions He was ... but he lost every penny when he invented Irish Goldfish.
Sage Why was that?
Onions They all drowned.
Sage Does he still invent things?
Onions No. He's dead. He drove his lorry off the White Cliffs of Dover to see if his air brakes worked. Anyway ... never mind about him. How are we going to move this overgrown duck?

Colin and Jill enter R *behind them*

Colin You're *not*.
Sage (*to Onions*) Hey, that was clever. I never even saw your lips move.
Jill What are you doing with Priscilla?

Sage and Onions turn, startled

Priscilla rises

Sage ⎫
Onions ⎬ (*together*) Ooo-er.
Colin Well?
Sage We ... er ... we were ... just taking her for a jog round the park.

Onions Yes. Trying to keep her fit.
Jill (*crossing to Priscilla*) Is this true, Priscilla?

Priscilla shakes her head

Sage Ooooh, you great big fibber.
Onions (*to the audience*) She's telling lies, isn't she, boys and girls?

Audience reaction

Colin (*grimly*) I suppose this is something to do with Uncle Clarence, isn't it? He can't get his hands on the golden eggs, so he decided to steal the goose that laid them.
Jill Thank goodness we managed to stop them in time. (*She takes the rope from round Priscilla's neck*)
Colin (*to Sage and Onions*) Now clear off, the pair of you. If I see you anywhere near Goose Grange again, I'll throw you into the nearest duck pond.

Sage and Onions scuttle off L

And now to deal with Uncle Clarence.
Jill (*to Priscilla*) Come on, Priscilla. Back to mother and a really special feed to make up for what's happened.

Harmony enters R

Colin (*startled*) An immortal.
Harmony   Alas, no longer on the Earth can dear Priscilla stay.
    To Fairyland she must return. Her golden eggs no more she'll lay.
Jill (*with dismay*) Oh, please . . . don't take her away from us. We don't care about the golden eggs. We love Priscilla for herself. Please let her stay. (*She hugs her*)
Harmony   There's nothing else that I can do, for so our Queen commands.
    Poor Mother Goose, our trust betrays, by falling into Discord's hands.
    She craves for beauty, grace and youth,
    And turns her back on love and truth.
    Why, even as we stand and speak, the Witch's Pool she goes to seek.
Colin Witch's Pool? What's that?
Harmony   If in its chilly waters she
    Should bathe . . . then beauty you will see.
    She'll be more fair of face than any mortal ever known.
    With soul as black as midnight sky, and heart as hard as stone.
Jill (*horrified*) Colin. We've got to stop her.
Colin (*to Harmony*) How can we find this Witch's Pool?
Harmony   Within the distant forest lies the haunted spot you seek.
    But mark my words . . . 'tis not a place for those whose nerve is weak.

> The trees have eyes ... and savage beasts bring fear with
>   drawn-out howl
> And Trolls and Demons there cavort with great Hobgoblins
>   foul.

Colin (*bravely*) They don't frighten *me*.

Harmony   If that be so, then there's a chance success will be your friend,
> And fortune unexpected all your efforts will attend.
> This feather from the magic goose your talisman shall be.
> (*She plucks a feather from Priscilla's back*)
> If victory tonight you gain, 'twill bring you straight to me.

Colin takes the feather

Jill But what if we're too late?

Harmony   Then Mother Goose is doomed, I fear ... which is Discord's
>   intent.
> Her only hope of saviour is her promise to repent.
> But quickly now. Your journey to the pool you must begin.
> For happiness, you battle.

Colin   And I promise you I'll *win*.

Harmony, Priscilla, Colin and Jill exit as ...

The Lights fade to Black-out

SCENE 3

Beside the Witch's Pool

An eerie glade in the middle of a sinister forest. The Witch's Pool is extended the full width of the glade, its banks of bulrushes and weeds hiding the water from view

The scene should be lit in blues and greens with great patches of shadow

When the scene begins, Discord and her evil spirits are performing a sinister dance. At the end of the dance Discord moves C

Discord Begone.

With much hissing and strange sounds, the creatures exit

> Come, Mother Goose and meet your fate.
> Your destiny right here doth wait.
> (*She gestures off* L)

Mother Goose enters, shivering with fright

Mother Goose Oh, what a creepy looking place. It's like (*she names a local football ground*) on a match day.

Discord   (*eagerly*) Quickly now. Brook no delay.
> Into the water straight away.
> (*She indicates the pool*)

Mother Goose Into the water? (*She moves up and peers into the pool*) You must be joking. I'm not sticking me tootsies into that lot. It's covered in weeds and frogspawn. Besides ... I'm not dirty. I had a bath two years ago. (*She moves back* DC)

Discord   Unless beneath this water deep
                  You plunge, your ugly face you'll keep.
                  The witching hour is almost here.
                  Take courage. Enter in, my dear.
                  (*She urges her towards the pool again*)

Mother Goose (*dithering*) Oh ... I don't know whether I should or not. Perhaps I've been imagining things. Maybe I'm not as ugly as I think I am.

Discord   You are. You are. Remember how folk mock?
                  Your face could stop an eight-day clock.

Mother Goose (*eyeing her suspiciously*) You seem very anxious to get me into that water, missis woman. I'm not too sure I should trust you. (*To the audience*) Do you think I should trust her, boys and girls?

Audience reaction

You see? The boys and girls don't trust you either.

Discord   (*snarling*) Bah ... they're simply jealous of the beauty
                  you'll receive
                  But please yourself. If *them* you're now intending to
                  believe.
                  I'll go ... but this I vow ... although for youthfulness
                  you crave,
                  You'll live in desperation and go ugly to your grave.
                  (*She turns to go*)

Mother Goose (*afraid*) No, no. Don't go. I'll do it. I'll do it.

Discord   (*turning back*) And into the Magic Pool you'll plunge?

Mother Goose   With cake of soap and Woolworth sponge.

(*Startled*) Good Heavens. Now *I'm* speaking verse. A very odd condition. What causes us to speak like this?

Discord It's pantomime tradition.

Mother Goose   If that's so ... here's another bit ere I drink from
                  beauty's cup.

Discord (*puzzled*) I'm not sure that I understand.

Mother Goose   One strip-tease ... coming up.

Discord reels back and exits as

Mother Goose launches herself into a rousing strip routine, tossing the discarded clothes offstage

At the end of the number she exits into the pool

We hear a loud splash

Discord enters L

Discord   The deed is done. Her soul is mine.
        I win the Fairy Crown.
        Though beauty she may gain, her world of dreams comes
         crashing down.

Discord gives a delighted laugh and exits DL

Clarence enters UR

Clarence (*fuming*) Marry Mother Goose? Me? Why the whole idea's ridiculous. She's as ugly as sin and so old if she put the correct number of candles on her birthday cakes, they'd be declared a fire hazard. It's no wonder she doesn't object to men who kiss and tell. At her age she's grateful for the publicity. Still . . . if everything went according to plan, the Magic Goose is locked in my cellar and soon I'll be the richest man in the world. (*He rubs his hands with glee*)

Colin (*off*) Mother Goose. Mother Goose.

Jill (*off*) Where are you?

Clarence Botheration. Here comes that stupid nephew of mine with his stuck-up girlfriend. What are *they* doing here in the middle of the forest? Surely they can't have discovered my little secret? I'd better hide till they've gone.

Clarence exits DL

Colin and Jill enter UR

Jill (*nervously*) I think we're here. (*She looks around fearfully*)

Colin Yes. That looks like the Witch's Pool, all right. But there's no sign of your mother.

Jill It's awfully gloomy here. I'm sure it must be haunted.

Colin (*laughing*) Pooh. There's nothing to be afraid of. Nothing can harm you while *I'm* here.

Jill I know . . . but I'd feel a lot safer if you put your arm around me.

He does so

 (*Worried*) If only we knew where mother was . . . and why she's so unhappy. I know she's not the prettiest woman in the world, but she *is* my mother and I love her exactly the way she is. So does Billy.

Colin Don't worry. As soon as she arrives here I'm sure we'll be able to sort things out. Then as soon as that's done, it's back to Goose Grange to begin the preparations for our wedding day.

Jill But what about Priscilla?

Colin Perhaps she'll be returned to us if we can only persuade your mother not to have anything to do with this Discord creature.

Jill I hope so. I can't bear the thought of never seeing her again.

Colin Well it's up to the Fairy Queen, but perhaps when we do get married, she'll allow Priscilla to at least come and visit us. After all . . . we'll have to introduce her to the children.

Jill Children?

Colin Oh, yes. We'll have a nice little cottage of our own ... two lovely children, and everything else we've ever dreamed of.

Jill I can hardly wait.

Colin and Jill sing

Song 13

At the end of the song, they wander off DL, *arms around each other*

As they exit, Sage and Onions come hurrying in UR

Sage That's torn it. We've lost them *all* now. There isn't a soul in sight.

Onions (*looking round, baffled*) I wonder where they've gone?

Sage Never mind about that. What are we going to tell the Squire?

Onions *I* don't know. You're the one with all the bright ideas.

Sage (*unhappily*) I don't *feel* very bright at the minute. I think we'd better just tell him the truth.

Clarence enters DL

Clarence The truth about *what*?

Sage Oo-er. (*Backing away*) Well ... it's like this, Squire ...

Clarence Yes. (*He glowers at him*)

Onions (*gulping*) We've lost Priscilla.

Clarence (*furiously*) What?

Sage (*quickly*) It wasn't our fault. Colin and Jill spotted us and took her back.

Clarence Dolts. Fools. Idiots. Didn't you try to stop them?

Onions Of course we did. We could have beaten them off with one hand tied behind our backs.

Clarence Then why didn't you?

Sage We couldn't find any string.

Clarence Bah. You incompetent oafs. You're fired. Without the Golden Goose I'm done for. I've spent almost every penny I had in trying to keep up with that ugly old faggot. The only way I'm going to get my hands on her money now is to *marry* her. (*He fumes*) Oooh, I'm so agrannoyed, I've a good mind to steal a packet of jelly babies and bite their heads off. Out of my way. I've got some serious thinking to do.

Clarence exits DR

Onions (*in disgust*) Huh. We might have guessed it'd all be our fault. Now we've no jobs again and we haven't a penny to spend between us.

Sage It's all getting too much for me. I spend hours every day worrying about being out of work. It makes me so ill I can't keep anything on my stomach.

Onions Ask the doctor for some pills, then.

Sage I did ... but they roll off during the night.

Onions Mind you, I never go to the doctors myself. A friend of mine told *his* doctor that he was getting very short-sighted, and all the doctor said was "Eat more carrots."

Sage What's wrong with that? Everybody knows carrots are good for your eyes. I mean . . . you never see a rabbit wearing spectacles, do you?

Onions I know . . . but the thing was . . . three months later he went out one night, fell over and broke his leg.

Sage What? Because he couldn't see?

Onions No. He tripped over his ears.

Sage (*spotting the teddy*) Hey . . . look. Somebody's left a teddy bear over there. Let's take it back to the village and sell it.

They approach the teddy

Audience reaction

Billy hurriedly enters DR

Billy Take your hands off my Teddy.

Sage and Onions quickly exit

Blimey . . . you can't trust them with anything, can you? First they try to pinch Priscilla, and now they try to pinch my Teddy. Just wait till I get my hands on them. Here . . . I bet you'll never guess where I've been? Go on. Have a guess. (*Audience reaction*) No . . . you're all wrong. I've been to join the Navy. I was so annoyed with my Mum for not giving me some money, I decided to run away to sea. I went into the recruiting office and I said to the man behind the counter, "Hey . . . Admiral . . . I want to join the Navy." He looked me up and down and said, "Can you swim?" I said, "Blimey . . . have you run out of boats." He said "Supposing the enemy ships were as thick as peas. What would you do?" I said, "Shell them." He said, "Have you ever been to a foreign country before?" I said, "Oh, yes. I went to Paris once. I saw the Eyeful Tower . . . the Champs de Elowise, *and* the Moolin Rooge. I even went into one of them naughty nightclubs that my father told me never to go in to in case I saw something I shouldn't." He said, "And *did* you see something you shouldn't?" I said, "Yes. I saw my dad." Anyway . . . I didn't join. I came back here to tell my Mum I was sorry for calling her names. 'Cos you shouldn't call your Mum names, should you? No. Of course not. The only trouble is, I don't know where she's got to.

We hear a raucous, brassy, rendering of "St Louis Woman" as

Mother Goose emerges from the Magic Pool. She is extravagantly made up in a figure-hugging gown and blonde, upswept wig, and glitters like a Christmas tree

(*Eyes popping*) Blimey . . . it's (*he names a well-known beauty*)

Mother Goose (*teetering* C) It worked. It worked. I'm the most beautiful girl in the world. (*She winks*) Now for a bit of fun. (*To Billy*) Hallo, big boy. (*She puckers her lips at him*) Come up and see me sometime.

Billy (*looking about him, startled*) Has somebody else come on?

Mother Goose (*to the audience: in delight*) He doesn't recognize me.

Billy (*to the audience*) Ooooooooh. My luck's changed.

Mother Goose (*vamping him*) Howdya like to *do* somethin' for me?

Billy (*drooling*) Ooooooh. I'd give you the shirt off my back.

Mother Goose (*to the audience*) Typical. The minute he thinks he's got me, he starts giving me his washing. (*To Billy*) Tell me, young man ... are you well-behaved?

Billy Not half. When I was a little boy, every time I did something really good, my dad used to give me a penny and a pat on the head.

Mother Goose (*to the audience*) By the time he was sixteen, he had twenty pounds in the bank and the flattest head in town. (*To Billy*) Come over here and join me.

Billy (*worried*) You're not coming apart, are you?

Mother Goose (*laughing archly*) No, no. But there's something I'd like to ask you.

Billy (*crossing to her*) Yes ... and there's something I'd like to ask *you*. What are you doing walking round these woods on your own? It's very dangerous in here, you know. Only five minutes ago I spotted a leopard.

Mother Goose (*pushing him playfully*) Don't be silly. That's the way they grow. Now tell me ... what do you think about your mother? (*She winks at the audience*)

Billy (*in surprise*) My mother? Well ... I think she's smashing. Why?

Mother Goose (*startled*) Eh? (*Recovering*) But she's very *ugly*, isn't she?

Billy (*indignantly*) No she isn't. She's beautiful.

Mother Goose (*pressing*) As beautiful as me?

Billy Oh ... no. She's far better looking than you.

Mother Goose But I hear she's very *bad-tempered*.

Billy She's nothing of the kind. She's the best Mum in the whole wide world and I wouldn't change her for anybody.

Mother Goose (*thrown off balance*) But ... but ... suppose she wanted to be *different*?

Billy How do you mean ... different?

Mother Goose Well ... let me put it this way. What's the opposite of misery?

Billy Happiness.

Mother Goose And the opposite of sadness?

Billy Gladness.

Mother Goose And the opposite of woe?

Billy Giddy-up.

Mother Goose (*pushing him*) Oh, you're as thick as two short planks.

Billy (*startled*) Here ... you sounded just like my Mum, then.

Clarence enters DR *and sees Mother Goose*

Clarence (*startled*) Good Heavens. It's the girl of my dreams.

Billy Here. Buzz off, you. This is *my* bird.

Mother Goose You know why they call us girls "birds", don't you, young man?

Billy No.

Mother Goose It's because of the *worms* we keep picking up.

Clarence (*gushingly*) Ah, dear lady ... could you ever learn to love a man like *me*?

Mother Goose Providing he wasn't *too* much like you.
Clarence (*passionately*) What would I have to give you to steal a kiss?
Billy Chloroform.

Sage and Onions enter

Sage (*seeing her*) Oh . . . it's the girl of my dreams.
Onions And mine.
Mother Goose (*peering offstage*) There must be a nest out there. (*To the audience*) Look at them, girls. Four men . . . and all madly in love with me. Who says it wasn't worth having the full treatment? (*To the men*) All right, boys. Let's hear it for Big Momma. Who's the most beautiful doll you've ever set eyes on?
All You are.

They sing with Mother Goose

Song 14

At the end of the song, Mother Goose is flanked by two men at each side of her. She gives a delighted laugh

Mother Goose And now I'll let you into a big secret. Would you like to know who I really am?
Men Yes. Of course, etc.
Mother Goose I'm Mother Goose. (*She beams*)

All react in disbelief

Billy (*goggling at her*) Mum?
Clarence Gasoline?
Mother Goose Clementine.
Clarence But that's ridiculous.
Mother Goose Not half as ridiculous as you lot. I bathed in the Magic Pool and turned into the ravishing creature you see before you. (*She preens herself*) Now what do you say to *that*?
Sage I don't believe it.
Onions Me neither.
Clarence (*recoiling*) You're nothing but a fraud. Mutton dressed as lamb.
Mother Goose Nothing of the kind. I'm a vegetarian.
Billy You look *terrible*. You're just a cheap chest of drawers covered in two coats of fresh paint.
Mother Goose (*stung*) How dare you? How very dare you? I don't know how you can look at your own mother in that tone of voice.
Billy (*upset*) You're not my mother. I never want to see *you* again. I want my *real* Mum back.

He bursts into tears and hurries off R

Clarence (*to Sage and Onions*) Come on you two. We're not staying here to be made fools of.

Clarence exits DL

Sage Painted hussy.

Sage follows Clarence off

Onions Jezebel.

Onions exits

We hear Discord's harsh laugh fill the stage

Mother Goose covers her ears and hides her face

The laughter fades and all is silent

Mother Goose (*stricken*) What have I done? I gave up everything to become
beautiful so people would like me . . . but now I am beautiful . . . nobody
wants me after all. (*She sniffles*) I've lost my family . . . I've lost my friends
. . . and worst of all . . . I've lost Priscilla. What a stupid, vain, ridiculous
old woman I really am. (*She sobs bitterly*) Why couldn't I have been
contented?

Harmony enters DR

Harmony	Poor Mother Goose. How bitter are The tears that now you shed. Your hopes and dreams are shattered.
Mother Goose	(*bitterly*) Oh, I wish that I were dead.
Harmony	Yet even in life's darkest hour, salvation can be waiting. If you repent, the spell you'll break. So come. No hesitating.

Mother Goose (*looking up hopefully*) You mean . . . I can go back to being
how I was before?

Harmony	If into yonder pool you plunge, your beauty you will lose. And once again you'll simply be, poor, homely, Mother Goose.
Mother Goose	Then stand aside. My mind's made up. I'm going straight back in. These looks of mine will now dissolve . . . like soluble asp'rin.

She dashes up to the pool and throws herself in

We hear a huge splash

Harmony	(*facing front*) Come sisters from our Fairy Dell. Let happiness hold sway. In joyous revel celebrate as Discord's spell is washed away. (*She waves her hand*)

Fairies stream into the glade dressed in myriad colours and shades

They perform a joyful ballet as

Harmony exits

15—Ballet

At the end of the dance, all exit

Jill and Colin enter

Jill We've walked all around the pool and there hasn't been a glimpse of her.

Colin She should have been here ages ago if Harmony was right.

Mother Goose (*off*) Oooooooooooh.

Jill (*frightened*) What's that? (*She clings to Colin*)

Colin It seemed to come from over there. (*He indicates the pool*)

Mother Goose (*off*) Ooooooooooooooooh.

Mother Goose staggers in clutching her head. She is wearing her old rags again as in scene one

Where am I?

Jill Mother. (*She hurries to her*)

Colin Mother Goose. (*Moving to her*) Thank goodness we found you in time.

Mother Goose (*dazed*) Eh? (*She clutches hold of Jill*) Do you recognize me?

Jill Of course we do. (*She puts her arm around Mother Goose*) Where on earth have you been? We were so worried about you.

Mother Goose Oh ... I've had a terrible dream. Really terrible. (*Lowering her voice*) I dreamed I was on a desert island with fifty hairy-chested muscle men who hadn't seen a woman for ten years.

Colin What's so terrible about that?

Mother Goose *I* was a man as well. Oh ... take me home. Back to my friends and family ... but most of all ... back to my darling Priscilla.

Jill I'm afraid we can't do that, mother. You see ... the Fairy Queen sent Harmony to take her back to Fairyland. It seems you gave Priscilla to the evil fairy Discord, and she has to be presented to her right away.

Mother Goose (*aghast*) Oh, no. I thought now I was back to normal, everything would be just as it was before. That we'd all be together again.

Colin I'm afraid not. When Priscilla returned to Fairyland, all the gold vanished with her. Goose Grange is only a ruin again.

Mother Goose You mean ... we're bankruptured?

Jill I'm afraid so.

Mother Goose Well ... *I* don't care. Who wants money, anyway? I've learned my lesson. If I never see another penny again I shall still be happy if I've got my family around me. (*Suddenly*) Here ... just a minute though. (*She turns and dashes back to the poolside*)

Jill (*with alarm*) Where are you going?

Mother Goose (*turning*) I've just remembered something. On my way out of the pool I banged my head on something. (*She bends over the rushes and lifts a battered old tin box up*)

Colin It's an old document box. Just like the one we used to have at home. What's in it?

Mother Goose I don't know, but I'm going to have a look. (*She comes* DC *with it, opens it and peers inside*) It's a piece of paper.

All gather round to read it

Colin It's my father's handwriting. (*He takes the paper and reads aloud*) "To my dear son Colin, I leave all my lands, money and titles, and to my wicked brother Clarence, nothing but the hope that when he comes out of prison he'll stay as far away from Merrilea as possible".

Mother Goose (*with amazement*) Well, I'll go to the foot of our stairs.

Jill (*with delight*) Oh, Colin. This means that *you're* the real Squire of Merrilea. Isn't it wonderful?

Mother Goose (*puzzled*) But how did it get into that pool?

Jill I've a good idea. Come on. We've got to tell everyone the news.

Colin No. Wait. There's time for that when we've dealt with Discord and rescued Priscilla. We have to get to Fairyland.

Mother Goose Eh? How do we do that?

Colin With the help of this magic feather. (*He displays it*) According to Fairy Harmony, we can be there before you can say Jack Robinson.

Mother Goose Well strike me pink.

A pink follow spot is turned onto her

Ooooooooh.

Colin Come on everyone. To the rescue of Priscilla.

The Lights quickly fade to Black-out

SCENE 4

A Quiet Street

Billy enters R *looking very dejected*

Billy Hiya, kids. Ooh, I aren't half fed-up. Me Mum's gone all funny peculiar, Jill and Colin have vanished, Goose Grange has tumbled down again and I've only got a pound left in my pocket. What am I going to do?

Sage and Onions enter L

Sage (*fed-up*) Hiya, Billy. You couldn't lend us a pound, could you? We want to get something to eat and we've only got a pound each.

Billy Well . . . I *could* . . . if you were both here. But as you're *not* . . . I can't.

Onions What do you mean, *if* we were here? We *are* here.

Billy No you're not. And I can *prove* it.

Sage Don't be daft. Of course you can't.

Billy All right, then. I bet you a pound that I can prove you're not here.

Sage
Onions } (*together*) You're on.

Billy Put your money down.

Billy and Sage both put one pound notes (or coins) down

Right. Now you're not in China, are you?

Sage
Onions } *(together, puzzled)* Course we're not.

Billy And you're not in the Antarctic, are you?

Sage
Onions } *(together, still puzzled)* No.

Billy Well if you're not in China . . . and you're not in the Antarctic . . . you must be somewhere else, mustn't you?

Sage
Onions } *(together)* Well of course we must.

Billy Then if you're somewhere else, you can't be here, can you? *(He picks up the money)* I win.

Billy exits R, laughing

Onions We've been diddled. Now we've only a pound left between us.

Sage Just a minute. Here comes Squire Creep. Let's play the same trick on him.

Clarence enter L

(Loudly) Oh, if only Squire Creep were here. He'd be able to make a little money.

Clarence Did someone mention my favourite after shave? *(He coughs)* Ahem. . . . Here I am.

Onions Oh, we were just talking about you. Here . . . we bet you a pound that we can prove you're not here.

Clarence But that's ridiculous. Of course I'm here. You're talking to me, aren't you?

Sage All the same . . . we can prove you're not here, and if we can't . . . you win a pound from us.

Clarence *(aside)* It's like stealing candy from a baby. *(To them)* Very well, then. I'll wager you a pound. What do I have to do?

The routine is repeated as before

Sage and Onions pocket the money and exit L laughing

Bah. I've been outwitted. I've got to get that money back. *(He looks offstage)* Aha . . . here comes Billy Goose. I'll try the same trick on him.

Billy enters R

Ah, William, my boy. I bet you the sum of one pound that I can prove you're not here. *(He beams)*

Billy *(after a knowing look at the audience)* I bet you can't.

Clarence Oh, yes I can. Put your money down.

They both put their money down

Now then . . . *(he titters)* He he he he.

Billy *(laughing with him)* He he he he he.

Clarence He he he he he.
Billy (*to the audience*) I can't stand comics who laugh at their own jokes.

The routine proceeds as before

At the end Clarence is convulsed with laughter at his triumph

Billy picks up the coins and begins to exit R

Clarence (*snapping out of it*) Here ... you're walking off with my money.
Billy No, I'm not, Squire. I'm not here.

  Billy dashes off, laughing

  Clarence angrily chases him

The Lights quickly fade to Black-out

SCENE 5

The Court of the Fairy Queen

*A throne room. The Fairy Queen is seated on her throne which is raised on a
small platform with a short flight of steps leading up to it. Fairies flank her at
each side. In the main body of the room, Babes and Juniors, dressed as geese
and goslings, are dancing. Two stern looking Goose Guards holding spears are
at each side of the stage*

16—Dance

At the end of the dance, the Fairy Queen stands

Geese and goslings fall back and kneel

Fairy Queen I thank you, dear subjects. A most pleasant entertainment. My
pleasure however is somewhat lessened by the news of a most unpleasant
occurrence.

All react in consternation

  This very day ... in great distress ... our beloved Priscilla has returned
  from Earth.

There is further reaction

  Although unharmed, it would appear that whilst on earth, she was sorely
  treated by one Mother Goose ... a wicked mortal who accepted her
  golden eggs willingly, yet gave her to Fairy Discord in exchange for
  earthly beauty.

There is a reaction of shocked disbelief from all

  Because of this Priscilla must now be presented to Discord with all due
  ceremony, and even the Royal Crown of Fairyland passes from my
  hands.

There is a further flurry of disbelief

Let Discord be admitted to my Court.

Discord appears DL *in triumph*

Discord (*laughing*) I said I'd prove you wrong, didn't I?
Fairy Queen   (*ignoring the remark*) From Fairy Throne, I now step
                         down.
                         To you, Discord, I yield my crown.
                         (*She begins to remove it*)

Harmony enters R *with urgency*

Harmony One moment, Your Majesty.

Everyone turns to look at her

I fear our sister Discord acts too quickly. Mother Goose and her two
champions are even now requesting entrance to our Realm.
Fairy Queen (*with outrage*) What? She dares to set foot on our enchanted
soil? (*To the Goose Guards*)
                         With beaks erect and quills a quiver,
                         Bring Mother Goose here . . . and anyone with 'er.

The Goose Guards exit quickly

Discord (*smirking*) It's much too late for you to interfere, dear Harmony. I
tempted her with beauty, so the Fairy Crown indeed is *mine*.
Harmony   Not so. Her better nature caused her quickly to repent,
                         And once again, she's old and worn, but *happy* and
                         content.
Discord (*shaken*) You lie. No one can withstand my insidious powers.

*Mother Goose, still shabby, Colin, Jill and the Goose Guards who menace
them with their spears, enter*

Mother Goose (*looking around in wonderment*) So this is (*she names a local
dance hall or nightclub*) Oh . . . (*she sees the Fairy Queen*) It's Margaret
Thatcher.
Fairy Queen (*coldly*) What brings you to our Royal Court?
Colin (*bowing*) Your Majesty. We come to right a dreadful wrong. By
means of magic and trickery, *that* evil creature (*he indicates Discord*) stole
Priscilla from poor Mother Goose.
Fairy Queen And who are you, young man?
Colin Colin, true Squire of Merrilea, Your Majesty.
Fairy Queen And this? (*She indicates Jill*)
Jill (*curtsying*) Jill, Your Majesty. Daughter of Mother Goose.
Fairy Queen (*frowning*) And who is *that*. (*She indicates the teddy*) Bring him
to me at once.

The Goose Guards head for the teddy

Audience reaction

Billy rushes in

Billy Get your beaks off my Teddy. (*To the audience*) Thanks, kids. (*He sees his mother*) Oooooh, Mum. You're back to normal again. (*He hugs her*)

Fairy Queen And who might *you* be, pray?

Billy I might be (*he names a well-known celebrity*) but I'm not. I'm Billy Goose ... my mother's deeply religious son.

Mother Goose (*startled*) Deeply religious? You?

Billy Yes. I'm a devout coward.

Fairy Queen (*frostily*) What do you want of us?

Mother Goose (*very humbly*) If it please Your Magneticals ... Your Royal Queenship I've come to say how sorry I am for what's happened, and to rescue poor Priscilla from that rotten old Fairy Harpsichord.

Discord (*harshly*) Never. The magic goose is mine.

Mother Goose (*fiercely*) Oh, no she isn't. You tricked me into parting with her in exchange for a face lift and a classy chassis ... but I changed my mind, my face, my wig and my frock in double quick time. I suddenly realized that looks aren't everything. (*Wryly*) In *my* case, they aren't anything. The only time I'm likely to get a chap on my hands is in the middle of a bad winter. But that's all beside the point. *No* face lift ... *no* goose. (*She glares defiantly at Discord*)

Fairy Queen Am I to understand you wish Priscilla to be returned to you, mortal?

Mother Goose No. You're not. (*Sadly*) I'd love to have her back ... more than anything else in the world ... but I don't deserve her. I betrayed her trust ... and yours ... so I don't deserve anything but to be poor and ugly for the rest of my life. But all the same ... Priscilla doesn't deserve *her*.

Billy Mum's right. She's a nasty, wicked old fairy. (*To the audience*) Isn't she kids?

Audience reaction

Fairy Queen You seem to think a lot of our dear Priscilla.

Mother Goose I do. She's the most beautiful goose that's ever lived and I'd do anything to help her.

Fairy Queen Even give your life?

There is a stunned reaction

Jill (*fearfully*) Mother. (*She holds her*)

Mother Goose (*drawing herself up*) If I have to. You can chop my head off and throw it in my face. All I want is for Priscilla to be free to do as she wants, and my family and friends to be sent back to earth in safety. (*She looks down awaiting judgement*)

Clarence, Sage and Onions enter L

Clarence (*sneering*) Oh, very touching. Very touching. You'll get an Academy Award for *that* performance. (*To the Fairy Queen*) But if anyone's going to get their hands on that goose, it's *me*. Bring her in at once.

Everyone gasps in amazement

Fairy Queen (*with annoyance*) And who are *you*?

Clarence Squire Creep. Rightful owner of the Magic Goose. She was found on my property and I insist on having her returned to me. So come on, twinkle-toes. Hand her over.

Colin (*stepping forward*) Just one moment, *Uncle* Clarence. Priscilla was found on *my* property, and *I'm* the rightful Squire of Merrilea. Mother Goose found the Will my father left, and handed it over to me.

Clarence Don't be ridiculous. She couldn't possibly have done. It's still at the bottom of the forest pool where I threw it ... (*he realizes*) Ooops.

Onions Oh, you naughty old man.

Sage You deserve to have the back of your legs slapped.

Fairy Queen Your crime shall be suitably punished, Master Creep, but first we have a much more important question to answer. To whom shall the Golden Goose belong? (*Firmly*) Summon her hither.

Priscilla enters looking downcast

> These mortals stories now we've heard.
> So come, Priscilla, magic bird;
> We wait upon your judgement true.
> Which owner would be best for *you*?

Discord (*eagerly*) Choose me. I'll give you the power to make people sad.

Clarence Choose *me*. A gold egg every morning and I'll feed you twice a week.

Mother Goose simply hangs her head

Priscilla looks from one to the other, then waddles to Mother Goose and snuggles up to her

Everyone but Discord and Clarence are delighted

Discord You *shan't* have her. You shan't.

Clarence She's *mine*.

Priscilla scrapes her foot on the floor in anger then lunges at Discord and Clarence. With cries of fear, Discord and Clarence are chased around the Court as everyone cheers. Priscilla chases them off then returns to Mother Goose and the others

Fairy Queen The choice is made. From henceforth, Discord is banished from Fairyland. Never again will her spiteful actions bring sorrow to the people of this realm.

All cheer

> Now, Mother Goose ... to deal with *you*.
> You've proved your worth ... and learned a lesson too.
> Though grass appears much greener behind another's
>   fence,
> There's nothing can replace content, good health and
>   common sense.
> The Magic bird we give to you, and each and ev'ry day.

If treated well and cherished, her golden eggs she *still* will
lay.

Mother Goose (*hugging Priscilla*) You don't have to worry about that,
Missis Queen. From now on, she'll never want for anything.

Fairy Queen   Then back to earth . . . where joyous celebration will hold
sway;

And this I vow . . . we'll all be there for Jill and Colin's
wedding day.

All cheer loudly

Optional finale song for all, then the scene ends in celebratory style

Scene 6

Back in Merrilea

Billy Goose entertains, or as required

Scene 7

The Ballroom at Goose Grange (as before)

*A short dance for Babes or Juniors may be inserted before the walkdown
commences, which, allowing for alteration depending on which group are used,
is as follows*:

    Babes
    Juniors
    Senior Chorus
    Fairy Queen
    Priscilla
    Sage and Onions
    Harmony and Discord
    Clarence Creep
    Billy Goose
    Mother Goose
    Colin and Jill

After everyone has taken their applause

Colin	Your kind applause has made the work we've done seem all worthwhile.
Jill	With dance and song, and possibly a laugh, a tear, a smile.
Billy	And now it's time to say "Goodnight", but before we turn you loose . . .
Mother Goose	Good Luck. Good Health and Happiness, from all in
Everyone	Mother Goose.

There is a reprise of the Finale song and then the Curtain *falls*

FURNITURE AND PROPERTY LIST

PROLOGUE

On stage: Floral bower, large golden book

Personal: **Fairy Queen:** glittering gown and silver crown (used throughout)

ACT I

Scene 1

On stage: Cottage with practical door

Off stage: Large gold eggs **(Billy)**

Personal: **Clarence:** riding crop, £5 note
Colin: stick with knotted bag, pound notes
Billy: large teddy bear, packet of cough sweets
Sage: hat
Mother Goose: apron, shopping bag. *In it:* pair of old, odd gloves
Harmony: wand (used throughout)

Scene 2

On stage: Nil

Personal: **Billy:** 20 pence coin, wad of pound notes
Clarence: small, foil-wrapped fish

Scene 3

On stage: Teacher's desk, large hand-bell, Dunce's cap, slap-stick cane, large blackboard and easel, chalks, eraser, two long school benches, short bench with one legless end, books

Personal: **Mother Goose:** teacher's cap and gown
Children: paper darts, conkers, pea-shooters, paper pellets, rulers, dolls, bubbles, skipping ropes

Scene 4

On stage: Nil

Personal: **Mother Goose:** fantastic, hideous gown

Scene 5

On stage: Nil

Off stage: Large mirror **(Men)**
              Flower garlands **(Fairies)**

Personal: **Footmen:** trays of drinks

ACT II

SCENE 1

On stage: Old statue of a nymph with the face partially chipped away, white garden
             seat, floral bower and roses

SCENE 2

On stage: Nil

Personal: **Priscilla:** rope around her neck

SCENE 3

On stage: Banks of bulrushes and weeds, battered old tin box (hidden from sight). *In
             it:* piece of paper

SCENE 4

On stage: Nil

Personal: **Billy:** one pound
             Sage: one pound
             Clarence: two pounds
             Onions: two pounds

SCENE 5

On stage: Throne on a raised platform

Personal: **Goose Guards:** spears

SCENE 6

On stage: As required

SCENE 7

On stage: As ACT I, SCENE 5

LIGHTING PLOT

Several simple interior and exterior settings

PROLOGUE

To open: Delicate pastel shade lighting on the floral bower

Cue 1	As the **Fairies** exit *Lights quickly fade to Black-out*	(Page 3)

ACT 1

To open: Bright sunny morning effect

Cue 2	As **Sage** and **Onions** exit *Lights dim*	(Page 8)
Cue 3	As **Discord** exits *Lights up on Mother Goose*	(Page 9)
Cue 4	**Mother Goose:** "Put the lights up, love, so I can get a better look at them." *House Lights up to full*	(Page 9)
Cue 5	**Mother Goose:** "Take 'em down again." *House Lights lowered*	(Page 9)
Cue 6	As **Sage** and **Onions** exit *Lights dim slightly*	(Page 12)
Cue 7	As **Harmony** and **Priscilla** enter *White spot on Harmony and on Priscilla*	(Page 12)
Cue 8	As **Harmony** exits *Fade white spot*	(Page 12)
Cue 9	As **Priscilla** exits *Fade white spot*	(Page 14)
Cue 10	At the end of Song 4 *Lights fade to Black-out*	(Page 16)
Cue 11	As SCENE 2 opens *Full general lighting*	(Page 16)
Cue 12	As **Jill, Colin** and the **Babes** exit *Lights fade to Black-out*	(Page 19)
Cue 13	As SCENE 3 opens *Full general lighting*	(Page 19)
Cue 14	As **Billy** is tipped onto the floor *Lights fade to Black-out*	(Page 25)

Cue 15	As SCENE 4 opens *Lights dim*	(Page 26)
Cue 16	As **Discord** exits *Lights brighten*	(Page 26)
Cue 17	As **Mother Goose** and **Clarence** exit *Lights fade to Black-out*	(Page 28)
Cue 18	As SCENE 5 opens *Full general lighting*	(Page 29)
Cue 19	As **Colin** and **Jill** exit *Lights dim*	(Page 30)
Cue 20	As **Discord** exits *Lights brighten*	(Page 30)
Cue 21	As **Discord** enters *Lights dim*	(Page 33)
Cue 22	As **Harmony** enters *White spot on Harmony*	(Page 34)
Cue 23	As **Harmony** waves her wand *Lights brighten*	(Page 35)

ACT II

To open: General daylight effect

Cue 24	As **Discord** enters *Lights dim*	(Page 41)
Cue 23	**Harmony:** "Greet Queen Discord on the morrow." *Lights quickly fade to Black-out*	(Page 42)
Cue 26	As SCENE 2 opens *Full general lighting*	(Page 42)
Cue 27	As **Harmony, Priscilla, Colin** and **Jill** exit *Lights fade to Black-out*	(Page 45)
Cue 28	As SCENE 3 opens *Green and blue lighting with great patches of shadow*	(Page 46)
Cue 29	**Mother Goose:** "Well strike me pink." *Pink spot on Mother Goose*	(Page 54)
Cue 30	**Colin:** "To the rescue of Priscilla." *Lights quickly fade to Black-out*	(Page 54)
Cue 31	As SCENE 4 opens *Full general lighting*	(Page 54)
Cue 32	As **Clarence** exits *Lights quickly fade to 'Black-out*	(Page 56)
Cue 33	As SCENE 5 opens *Full general lighting*	(Page 56)

EFFECTS PLOT

ACT I

No cues

ACT II

Cue 1	As **Mother Goose** exits into the pool *Loud splash*	(Page 46)
Cue 2	**Billy:** "... I don't know where she's got to." *Raucous, brassy, rendering of "St Louis Woman"*	(Page 49)
Cue 3	As **Mother Goose** throws herself into the pool *Loud splash*	(Page 52)

MADE AND PRINTED IN GREAT BRITAIN BY
LATIMER TREND & COMPANY LTD PLYMOUTH

MADE IN ENGLAND